ASSERTIVENESS

How to Stand Up for Yourself and Still Win
the Respect of Others

By
Judy Murphy

Thank you for reading.
Visit ScaredCocoon.com/free to download your bonus book:

Assertive at Work: Thriving in a Workplace of Mind Games and Bullies

Availability is limited, so
download today before it is gone tomorrow.

ISBN-10: 1495446859

ISBN-13: 978-1495446856

TABLE OF CONTENTS

INTRODUCTION

Opportunity does not knock; it presents
itself when you beat down the door.
—Kyle Chandler

Are you having a hard time saying "no" to others? Do you feel as though you can't offer your real opinion on topics because it may create conflict? Do you lack the courage to speak up for yourself? If so, you may be suffering from low self-esteem and lack assertiveness. It's not uncommon to feel this way, but if you'd like to learn more about how to better express yourself, you're in the right place. This book is designed with clear and simple instructions to improve your understanding of assertiveness and to help you employ its methods to enhance your communication.

Assertiveness is a style of communication that empowers its users to speak out and stand up for themselves in clear, respectful ways. It allows for the confident expression of your needs and feelings without the need for proof. Being assertive means expressing your wants while being mindful of the opinions, wants and feelings of others.

Assertiveness is critical for feeling empowered in your own mind as well as at work and at home. It's saying honestly to yourself and others, "This is who I am. This is how I want to be treated," while respecting other people's rights and opinions. Assertiveness isn't about being liked all the time, nor about making sure everyone is happy. It is about standing up for your right to be treated fairly.

There are many advantages to assertiveness. First, it empowers you to become a stronger communicator. It gives you confidence and enhances your self-esteem. Furthermore, it helps you gain others' respect while improving your decision-making skills. Most importantly, assertiveness serves as a way to reduce the bitterness you feel when your needs and wants aren't met.

In addition, the more assertive you become, the better able you are to face problems or conflicts with poise and a clearer head. It encourages you to make decisions without second-guessing yourself. You'll have more self-respect, and in return, will earn the respect of others. Feelings of being ignored or coerced will be replaced by feeling understood and in control of your decisions.

Assertiveness vs. Aggressiveness

When people think of assertiveness, they usually think of aggressiveness. Although it is common to mistake or confuse the two, they are very different. The delineation can be summarized with a simple word, *respect*.

Assertive people respect others' opinions, feelings, needs and wants. They do not place others' desires above their own. Instead, they find methods to avoid infringing upon people's rights while asserting their own rights and seeking compromise. It is possible to communicate your feelings without making someone feel that they must give in to you.

Aggressiveness, on the other hand, lacks respect. Aggressive people do not show respect to others. They are quick to shout or threaten people and invade their personal space. These individuals are so concerned with expressing their opinions that they will make a scene to be heard.

Aggressive behavior is characterized by a complete disregard for others' needs, wants, feelings or even personal safety. People who conduct themselves this way tend to stand up for themselves quickly, even if it means stepping on others. It is usually an angry, demanding behavior where voices are raised and where sarcasm can become threatening or violent. Conflicts with aggressive people turn into shouting matches that can segue into physical violence.

Over-aggressiveness and self-promotion seem rampant in the media and society today. People communicate aggressively every day while ignoring others' feelings and rights. Fights occur daily on talk shows, and the most obnoxious, aggressive person often gets the most air time on TV. Master manipulation has become a form of high art, sucking the life out of meaningful, respectful interactions.

On the contrary, assertiveness carries with it a quiet dignity. It isn't pushy like aggressive communication. It's about finding just the right balance of saying "no" to others while saying "yes" to you. Assertive people have the maturity and self-control to know what they want and how to get it without infringing on others' rights.

Being aggressive isn't likely to win you many friends, and ultimately, it may not get you what you want. Being assertive, on the other hand, allows you to set boundaries to express honestly how you want to be treated. The balance of self-confidence and finding a voice to express your needs and desires clearly can be refreshing, both to you and others.

Assertiveness vs. Passiveness

On the opposite end of the spectrum is passiveness. Passive communication assumes that others will understand what you want or need, even if you don't specify those needs. Silence and assumption are the hallmarks of this style.

The key difference here is again *respect*. Aggressiveness is defined by a lack of respect for others, while passiveness is defined by a lack of respect for one's self. Passive people disregard their own opinions, feelings, needs, and wants. They have a habit of placing their desires below others.

Assertive people never lose sight of the idea of self-respect. They respect themselves and use their words and actions to express the boundaries of what they need and want in a calm, clear voice while maintaining a posture that conveys confidence and composure.

As with aggressiveness, passivity isn't likely to win you many friends either. Worse, it is even less likely to get you what you want. Passiveness takes away the power of a person who stays quiet or just allows others to decide what needs to happen.

Assertive people are neither submissive nor aggressively dominant. They strike a clear balance of respect for others' opinions while stating their needs and wants in a way that cannot be misinterpreted. Because this style of communication is based on mutual respect, it's a diplomatic way to discuss issues ranging from how you want others to treat you to how you are willing to handle conflict.

Mark Caine said, "The first step toward success is taken when you refuse to be a captive of the environment in which you first find yourself." That is the premise of this book. It seeks to develop your skills as an assertive communicator to end your captivity. It will help you self-evaluate, recognize who you are and what you want, then give you simple, yet effective steps to find your voice so you can stand up for your wants and needs. You'll be better equipped to build the environment you want to live in by creating boundaries of respect for yourself while appreciating others' needs and wants.

Now, there is no shortage of assertive training books on the market today. Although I believe these books have good intentions and are sincere in wanting to give beneficial advice, they fail in a major way. They provide guidance that sound good in theory, but don't translate well in the real world.

This book tackles assertiveness from a different perspective. It does not present theory or suggestions that merely make you feel good in the moment. Nor does it sugar coat issues or always take the politically correct route. It examines assertiveness from a realistic point of view and provides real guidance for real people with real challenges.

If you are ready for this kind of change, it's time to start knocking down the doors that are presented to you, whether you've created them or someone has forced them upon you.

Before reading further, please make sure to grab your free book *Assertive at Work: Thriving in a Workplace of Mind Games and Bullies*. You can download the free copy at www.ScaredCocoon.com/free.

CHAPTER 1 - HOW DO YOU SEE YOURSELF?

To know oneself,
one should assert oneself.
—Albert Camus

To begin, it helps to first understand how you see yourself. This means looking at who you are, what you believe about yourself, and where you think you fit in the social hierarchy.

Understanding these things is important because they affect your ability to communicate assertively. For instance, if you see yourself in a negative light, you will have difficulty standing up for yourself. You may feel intimidated when asked a direct question or for your opinion. You may even lack the confidence to look someone squarely in the eye when speaking to them. Asking for clarification about a policy at work may be only slightly less painful than a heart attack.

In addition, with a limiting self-perception, you may focus too heavily on negative traits. Thoughts such as, "I'm not very good at handling conflict," "I don't feel comfortable saying no to someone in authority," or "I don't know how to ask for what I want," may reverberate in your mind each time you're faced with a situation in which you need to trust yourself. Your self-doubt may cause you to remain silent in confused self-preservation, preventing you from effectively expressing your needs and wants.

This can be illustrated in Kathryn Stockton's novel *The Help*, which focuses on the lives of African American maids working in white households in the segregated south of the 1960's. In several touching scenes, the main character, Aibelene, gently tells her young charge, Mae Mobley, "You is kind. You is smart. You is important," something the child's own mother would never tell her. The irony is that Aibelene doesn't believe those same things about herself. She is afraid to make eye contact with her employer, walks with a pained gait, and certainly doesn't stand up to the unreasonable demands she faces from the family for whom she works.

This passive character does not see herself in high regard. As a result, she is unable to be assertive. She lets others talk down and walk all over her. Aibelene's self-perception prevents her from effectively standing up and speaking out.

Self-Evaluation

To understand how your perception is affecting you, let's begin with a self-evaluation. Below we present two tests: one is a quiz and another is a hypothetical scenario. The quiz will give you a better understanding of what is going on for you internally, which will establish whether or not you have assertiveness issues and to what extent. The scenario will assess your communication skills, gauging your ability to interact with people. Take some time to reflect on each question so you can answer them as truthfully as possible.

Self-Evaluation Quiz

1. Begin with your level of eye contact. Do you look people in the eye when speaking with them? If you can't remember a single facial feature or their eye color, it's likely you are looking anywhere but in their eyes.

2. Now consider your voice. Do you project yourself clearly? If you are often asked to speak more loudly or to repeat what you've said, you probably speak quietly or mumble.

3. Do you speak confidently? Stumbling through conversations with "ums" and "uhs" doesn't communicate confidence.

4. Look at your stance and then your body when seated. How is your posture? Do you slouch or look down?

5. Looking internally, are you able to ask questions when you need clarification?

6. Do you feel comfortable around others?

7. Are you able to say "no" when you don't want to do something?

8. Are you able to express annoyance or anger appropriately?

9. Do you offer an opinion on a topic when you don't agree with someone?

10. Do you defend yourself against mistakes that aren't your fault?

After taking some time to truthfully respond to each question, review your answers. Notice how many questions to which you answered "no."

If you answered "no" to 2-3 questions, you are likely a self-assured and reliant person. Although you experience difficulty here and there, compared to the average person, asserting your needs and wants is not a challenge. If you in fact experience challenges, they may be due to your specific approach rather than an inherent inability to act assertively. It is possible you are coming off aggressive rather than assertive. We will address correct ways to approach assertive behavior.

If you answered "no" to 4-6 questions, there is a high chance you see yourself in a negative light. As a result, you experience more difficulty than the average person in communicating your needs and wants. While you may assert yourself on occasion, it is a test of will for you. You often second-guess your decision to act and replay numerous what-if scenarios before acting.

If you answered "no" to 7 or more questions, you have significant difficulty in this area. Not only do you doubt that you are worthy of respect, but you probably see yourself lower than others in the social totem pole. Even though you yearn to stand up for yourself, you never do. You always back down, coming up with reasons or excuses as to why backing down was the rational choice.

When you lack assertiveness, you do not live life on your own terms. Instead you let others take advantage of you and run your life. Non-assertive adults don't know how to say "no," which overburdens their schedules as well as their mental well-being.

Self-Evaluation Scenario

Let's look at another self-evaluation. Let's say that you really want to go on a trip. You don't want to go alone, so you are thinking about inviting your friend Julie. How would you approach asking her?

The assertive person will present the idea clearly and with respect for his or her friend. The person may approach it like this: "Hey Julie, I could really use a vacation because I'm feeling like I need some pampering. I would love to go somewhere tropical in the spring and enjoy the beach and some hiking with you. Would you be interested? Could you please check your schedule to see if you'd be available?" This dialogue is respectful, yet full of information about your wants (vacation, beach time, and hiking) and needs (the time of year you're available and your need to feel pampered).

The overly aggressive person might say this: "Julie, I'm booking my vacation for the beach next week. I want you to go, but you'll need to let me know right away if you can come. I've already picked a hotel by the beach for the second week in May. You'll need to pay me your half up front and book your own airline ticket." None of this dialogue would put Julie in a vacation mood. She'd probably feel more like a hostage on this getaway since all decisions have been taken out of her hands.

11

A passive person might approach the same situation this way: "Julie, I've been thinking about a vacation. Don't know if you'll want to go, but I guess the beach would be ok. Let me know if you can go." This conversation would probably make Julie feel as though she's the last person on Earth you want on your vacation. She's also not likely to know where or when to go. She will probably be left feeling that it's now up to her to plan your vacation together, and you'll just be along for the ride.

Again, what would your normal approach be to the situation? Would it be that of a passive person or would it be that of an overly aggressive person? If you see yourself as not worthy of people's time, they aren't likely to listen to you when you do speak up. If you see yourself as better than someone else, you're likely to discount their opinions and push your agenda right over theirs.

Assertive behavior never loses sight of respect for others. It allows for a balance of expressing your needs while respecting others' needs. If you really want that vacation with Julie, the best way to get it is to set boundaries about what you want and respect her wants, too. Besides, if Julie's truly your friend, you'll want honesty between the two of you. Though it may sound overly simplistic, the Golden Rule of "Do unto others as you would have done to you" is a perfect way to approach assertive communication.

From the above quiz and scenario, determine where you stand as it relates to how you perceive yourself. Do you see yourself in low regard? Are you overly passive? Do you expect others to make decisions for you? Do you have holes in your boundaries that people exploit?

If so, then you have to first change your self-perception. You need to change it from weak to strong. To be an assertive communicator, you must stand on a strong foundation of self and have the view that you are a person worthy of respect. If you don't have a strong foundation to stand on, assertive communication will not work for you.

Building a Strong Foundation

In this section, we examine two ways to develop a healthy self-perception. We start by establishing your rights. Then we help you improve your beliefs about who you are and the value you bring. Together, these two will make you feel more secure about who you are and your rights as a person. They will provide the positive support you need to ease into the assertive process.

"Bill of Rights" of Assertiveness

The "Bill of Rights" of assertiveness, from Manuel J. Smith's book When I Say No, I feel Guilty is a set of rules that gives you internal fortitude and serves as a reminder that you are worthy of respect. Shifting your mindset and using these rights as boundaries will allow you to assess your needs and wants calmly. It will help remove many of the passive feelings like guilt, doubt, and fear that can cause you to second-guess your decisions or actions:

Assertive Right 1: I have the right to judge my own behavior, thoughts and emotions and to take the responsibility for their initiation and consequence. The behavior of others may have an impact upon me, but I determine how I choose to react and/or deal with each situation. I alone have the power to judge and modify my thoughts, feelings and behavior. Others may influence my decision, but the final choice is mine.

Assertive Right 2: I have the right to offer neither reason nor excuse to justify my behavior. I need not rely upon others to judge whether my actions are proper or correct. Others may state disagreement or disapproval, but I have the option to disregard their preferences or to work out a compromise. I may choose to respect their preferences and consequently modify my behavior. What is important is that it is my choice. Others may try to manipulate my behavior and feelings by demanding to know my reasons and by trying to persuade me that I am wrong, but I know that I am the ultimate judge.

Assertive Right 3: I have the right to judge whether I am responsible for finding solutions to others' problems. I am ultimately responsible for my own psychological well-being and happiness. I may feel concern and compassion and good will for others, but I am neither responsible for nor do I have the ability to create mental stability and happiness for others. My actions may have caused others' problems indirectly; however, it is still their responsibility to come to terms with the problems and to learn to cope on their own. If I fail to recognize this assertive right, others may choose to manipulate my thoughts and feelings by placing the blame for their problems on me.

Assertive Right 4: I have the right to change my mind. As a human being, nothing in my life is necessarily constant or rigid. My interests and needs may well change with the passage of time. The possibility of changing my mind is normal, healthy and conducive to self-growth. Others may try to manipulate my choice by asking that I admit error or by stating that I am irresponsible; it is nevertheless unnecessary for me to justify my decision.

Assertive Right 5: I have the right to say "I don't know."

Assertive Right 6: I have the right to make mistakes and be responsible for them. To make a mistake is part of the human condition. Others may try to manipulate me, having me believe that my errors are unforgivable, that I must make amends for my wrongdoing by engaging in proper behavior. If I allow this, my future behavior will be influenced by my past mistakes, and my decisions will be controlled by the opinions of others.

Assertive Right 7: I have the right to be independent of the good will of others before coping with them. It would be unrealistic for me to expect others to approve of all my actions, regardless of their merit. If I were to assume that I required others' goodwill before being able to cope with them effectively, I would leave myself open to manipulation. It is unlikely that I require the goodwill and/or cooperation of others in order to survive. A relationship does not require 100 percent agreement. It is inevitable that others will be hurt or offended by my behavior at times. I am responsible only to myself, and I can deal with periodic disapproval from others.

Assertive Right 8: I have the right to be illogical in making decisions. I sometimes employ logic as a reasoning process to assist me in making judgments. However, logic cannot predict what will happen in every situation. Logic is not much help in dealing with wants, motivations and feelings.

Logic generally deals with "black or white," "all or none," and "yes or no" issues. Logic and reasoning don't always work well when dealing with the gray areas of the human condition.

Assertive Right 9: I have the right to say "I don't understand."

Assertive Right 10: I have the right to say "I don't care."

As a child, you were probably given things based on your behavior. Good manners may have garnered an extra smile or perhaps a favorite treat from adults. If, however, you were taught that good manners meant never saying "no" or questioning others, you may have carried that mindset into your adult life.

By emphasizing these "Bill of Rights" in your mind, you will begin to understand yourself and the mental walls you've created over the years more completely. You will realize you don't always have to say "yes" or have all the answers. Knowing this will give you the courage to stand assertively.

The limits that have made you a passive communicator can be removed here and now. Use these rights as a step towards respect for your own needs and wants. Being a person who isn't very assertive doesn't mean that you don't have valuable things to say. It only means that you need to work on finding your voice to say them. The above "Rights" give you that voice.

Self-Talk

Another way to develop a strong foundation of self is through the use of positive self-talk. If you've never heard of self-talk, it is the dialog that goes on inside your head. It is the conversation that you have with yourself on a daily basis. You use self-talk to think about things, to evaluate decisions, and to have discussions with others and yourself.

Interestingly, studies suggest that 80% of the discussions we have with ourselves about ourselves are damaging. We echo comments like "I am stupid," "I can't do anything right," or "Nothing ever goes my way." When you say, hear, or think these statements, you are in effect seeding your unconscious with ideas that take root and grow into a negative and restrictive self-perception. As you learned, it's this limiting perception that prevents people from having the confidence and courage to stand up. Negative self-talk creates a negative self-perception which hinders one's ability to be assertive.

To change your self-perception, you need to change your self-talk. That means talking to yourself in a way that empowers you, not in a way that takes away your power. Reverberate in your mind that you are in fact good enough. When you do, you will gain the inner force to uphold your rights.

To do this, first get rid of your negative self-talk. Stop saying harmful things about yourself to yourself. Imagine that you are a traffic officer and your job is to catch discouraging thoughts from entering the highway of your mind. Put the brakes on these thoughts and keep them from coming in.

Next, repeat statements that are positive and encouraging. You want not only to stop the negative, but also to start affirming the positive. Affirm words that promote a strong and healthy self-esteem. Doing this will plant new seeds in your mind, seeds that will eradicate the old messages and stem forth a stronger self.

To get you started, below is a list of 14 positive statements. They are designed both to develop your self-esteem and encourage you to stand up and speak out. Go through each statement and repeat them out loud or in your mind.

- I am a strong, confident communicator.

- I am worthy and deserving of respect.

- I easily express my thoughts, opinions, and desires.

- I stand up for my rights.

- I feel safe and secure about asking for what I want or need.

- I easily ask for what I want and effortlessly exercise my right to say no.

- It's my right to say "no," and I exercise this right when I need to.

- I allow myself to receive from others.

- I am important, my views are important, and my life is important.

- I trust and believe in myself.

- I feel for other people, but it is not reason to be taken advantage of.

- I am in control.

• I am comfortable in tense and difficult social situations.

• I don't let people and outside influences destabilize me.

Notice the internal shift you experience when affirming the statements. They give you a stronger inner voice and a sense of empowerment.

To encourage you to use self-talk, I would like to say that from experience, I've noticed that most people who are looking to become assertive are looking for a *magic pill*. In fact, most people looking for any type of change or solution are looking for this. They are hoping that they can simply read a book, attend a seminar, or take a pill and magically transform into a new person or have their problems solved. I believe most people reading this book are looking for this.

Unfortunately, life doesn't work this way. There are no magic pills or quick fixes. To become an assertive individual, you have to put in the effort. You have to take what you learn, whether it is from this book or elsewhere, and apply it in your life. You have to try, fail, figure out what works in different situations, and what doesn't. More importantly, you have to go out and experience what it is like to take assertive action.

Nevertheless, if you were hoping for a magic pill, the closest thing that comes to that is self-talk. By applying the statements like the above regularly in your life, you'll naturally become a more assertive individual. You'll find yourself growing into the kind of person who feels little apprehension asserting his or her needs. It will remove much of the struggle one experiences in the growth process. You won't have to think much about what to do nor how. Instead, you will find yourself spontaneously doing it. At times, it can seem magical.

However, you have to affirm the statements. I recommend affirming each sentence 10 times, twice a day. Do this once in the morning, before getting out of bed, and once in the evening, as you are falling asleep. The standard is to follow a routine for 30 days. Do it, however, for as long as you need or for as long as you derive benefit. When affirming the statements, feel free to change them to fit your situation and needs as well as the problems you are experiencing.

If you would like to learn more about self-talk, a good book on the topic is Self-Talk Your Way to Success. It is an informative guide that illustrates the theory behind self-talk and its practice.

In the next chapter, you will learn the building blocks needed for the meshing of your internal perceptions and external perceptions. You'll learn about how your body language and your conversational language speak volumes about you.

CHAPTER 2 - HOW DO OTHERS SEE YOU?

Assertiveness is not what you do,

it's who you are!

—Shakti Gawain

In the previous chapter, we explained that how you see and perceive yourself determines your ability to assert yourself. We also discussed ways to improve your self-perception to gain the confidence and self-worth necessary to be assertive. In this chapter, we will discuss how people's perception of you affects your ability to communicate. We will also discuss actions you can take to improve how others perceive you so they respond positively to your assertive communication.

People's perception of you has a profound effect on how they will treat you. If people see you as a weak person, they will treat you poorly. They will not give you the respect that you think you deserve or so desire. In fact, some people may even take advantage of you simply because they think they can get away with it.

Conversely, if people see you as a strong person, more often than not, they will treat you as someone worthy of respect, and they will give you that respect. They won't try to take advantage of you. At times, they will even go out of their way to please you to ensure they are on your good side.

So how does someone know to perceive you as a strong or weak person? How can someone tell whether or not you are worthy of respect? The answer is simple. They determine it through your body language.

Body language is a form of non-verbal communication that uses posture, gestures, eye movement and other facial expressions. They are signals that we send unconsciously that people are able to read. The keyword here is that the communication is non-verbal. Body language doesn't require you to say anything; the communication is made entirely by your physical appearance and/or demeanor.

For example, when someone is angry, you can easily tell. When someone is sad, you know. These people do not have to come out and say that they are angry or sad; you can see it in their expression and behavior. The same can be said of your self-worth. Through body language, people can quickly and instantly make judgments about who you are and your level of self-respect.

It is amazing just how much influence body language has on people's judgment. If you approach and talk to someone using one form of body language, they will judge you a certain way. If you approach the same person, but your body language is different, the perception they form will be entirely different. It's the same individual, but the perception is changed. To an extent, it does not matter how old you are, what you look like, or how much you have in your bank account. Your body language determines how people will see you, and consequently, how they will treat to you.

For example, if you approach someone while slouching or hunching your shoulders, barring a physical reason, you will leave the impression that you literally feel the weight of the world on you. This will make the other party feel uncomfortable and cause them either not to want to talk to you or to take advantage of you. If your eyes are cast downward, it will give the impression that you are dishonest, causing them to treat you as if you have something to hide. If you act insecure and shy, people will dismiss you and think you lack the merit to be taken seriously.

Often, this is done unconsciously, and those responding to you don't realize that they are responding to you differently. The person you are interacting with will simply react based on what your body language is projecting. Again, if it is projecting weakness, their response will be in accordance with that. If you are projecting confidence, your outcome will be entirely different.

The bottom line is this: People treat you based on how they perceive you, and their perception is formed through body language. Thus in order to communicate assertively, you need to present body language that projects strength and esteem, both with your voice and your physical demeanor. By doing so, you tell people "This is who I am. I am worthy of your respect. I have worthwhile opinions."

Developing Body Language

Below we will work to help you develop assertive body

language. The Rights of Assertiveness and Self-talk in the previous chapter served to help you become more assertive internally. The following exercises will work in much the same way, but to help you become more assertive externally. When you present yourself as physically confident, you garner others' attention. This makes it easier to achieve your objective because your presence says, "I have something important to say. Pay attention, please."

Walk the Walk

As mentioned, body language includes both your physical demeanor and voice. In this section we will work on your physical demeanor. We will discuss how to stand, gesture, look, and smile when communicating. We begin the discussion with your eyes.

Eyes

Eyes are often called the "windows to the soul," and with good reason. When someone looks into your eyes, they can often spot even the subtlest emotions. Do you return others' eye contact or look away often? If you are unable to maintain eye contact, your conversational partner is likely to feel that you're not interested in what he or she is saying. Worse yet, the person may mistrust you because it gives off the impression that you have something to hide.

Since assertiveness helps establish trust and mutual respect, maintaining appropriate eye contact is vital. It tells other people that you have a strong sense of self and are worthy of respect. Strong eye contact does not imply that you stare at them intensely or for long periods of time. It is about making a connection through your eyes that respectfully tells them you mean what you're saying and understand what they're saying.

To develop your ability to maintain eye contact, practice in the mirror. When you look at yourself in the mirror, find your pupils and notice your eye color. This will be a good way in the future to help you look at others. Remind yourself that you want to know their eye color (if you're close enough to see it). Don't over exaggerate by opening your eyes wide, which says that you're surprised or believe the other person is not telling the truth. On the opposite end, don't narrow your eyes too much either. Instead, relax your eyes and keep a natural demeanor. This will help you maintain a softer look than narrowing or widening your eyes, which conveys that you're either suspicious or aggressive.

Now, practice introducing yourself while maintaining the eye contact. Put your hand out in the mirror as if you are about to move into a hand shake and say: "Hi, my name is _____. How are you?" Hold eye contact for a couple of seconds as they respond.

This exercise will help you become more comfortable making eye contact with others. In the beginning this may feel awkward, but the more you practice, the more comfortable you will get. The more comfortable you are in front of the mirror, the more comfortable you will be when performing in front of a real person.

Smile

Your smile may or may not be your favorite feature, but it can become someone else's favorite thing about you if it is genuine. Remember that assertive communication is respectful. An honest, genuine smile that doesn't appear forced conveys that you respect the other person, and in return, helps the other person give respect to you. This is not the time to give a huge toothy grin or a tight smirk. Your honesty will show through and perhaps even put others at ease. When you assert yourself confidently, your smile reflects it. Say, "I'm so glad to meet you," and mean it while you look in their eyes. Then smile.

Shoulders

Shoulders that are back and relaxed open up your chest and project the image that you are confident and open to others. It's easy to improve your shoulders with a simple shrug and roll. To do this, lift both shoulders up as high as you can with your arms at your side. Roll them backwards and let them fall naturally as you relax. Take a deep breath.

Notice that your chest is more open and your neck and shoulders less tight. You've also just physically opened up your demeanor, telling others that you are receptive to conversation and that you feel comfortable with yourself. Relaxing your shoulders and standing up straight will do more than change your appearance; you will literally breathe easier.

Posture

The way you stand or sit can give the overall impression of physical confidence. Standing erect with your head up projects an image of assertiveness. The same goes with sitting. Sitting straight and tall in a chair with your feet on the ground gives you a stronger bearing and allows you to focus on your conversation. Stand or sit with your feet slightly apart and facing forward. This will help you feel as though you're literally on solid ground as you express your needs and wants.

A good exercise is to pretend you have a crown on your head. Place an invisible crown on top. There. Do you notice you're standing a little straighter or sitting a little taller? You would not be able to hold the crown up if you were looking down with poor posture. Practice walking while keeping your imaginary crown on top. You could certainly practice with a piece of paper, or for even more effect, a paper crown.

Hands

Hands can be wonderful tools for expression. People who are assertive communicators are able to gesture comfortably and occasionally. Passive communicators may shove their hands into their pockets or cover their mouth with them, even while speaking. Aggressive communicators may point at others or gesture grandly. It's best to relax your hands by your side. At times, you may need to point at a fact on a paper or board, but you should never point directly at someone to communicate assertively.

If you're having trouble with what to do with your hands when asserting yourself, hold a piece of paper or pen. This simple prop can give you a solid item to calm yourself while allowing you to focus on your physical demeanor and words. The only rule is to hold whatever prop you have quietly in your hands. You don't want to distract the person with whom you're speaking.

These are the important things to consider as it relates to body language. The above-mentioned exercises can be performed quickly and privately almost anywhere. Consider these steps as a physical reminder to be more assertive from head to toe. Practice them before you go out the door in the morning. Take a break before the big meeting at work and reset yourself physically. When you walk out confidently, you'll be ready when opportunities for assertiveness arise.

Now, let's now move to your voice.

Talk the Talk

In the 1999 movie *Office Space*, the character of Milton is an overworked, unappreciated employee practically invisible to everyone he works with. He is shuffled to progressively smaller cubicles and then finally to the office building's basement with the surplus filing cabinets. It's revealed that Milton's actually been removed from the company's payroll, yet he still comes in to work and tells people, "I believe you have my stapler" while they ignore him. Although the character provides some of the best comedy in the movie, he serves as a perfect example of a person who lacks assertiveness. His whining, mumbling voice utters, "Excuse me" over and over again while his boss and others talk right over him.

While Milton may be an over exaggeration of a passive communicator, the point of introducing him is to illustrate how one's voice—what a person says and how he or she says it—can cause a downward spiral in people's lives. If you lack self-respect, it will show in your word choice and tone, and others will not likely give you the respect you crave. Talking the talk means using language effectively to explain your needs and wants to others in no-nonsense terms.

To start, consider what others hear when you speak. Not just the words you say, but how you say them. If your voice is hard to hear, this forces others to have to work harder to comprehend you, which isn't a respectful use of their time. No one wants you to shout, but you should be able to speak in a normal tone, even if the subject isn't comfortable for you. If you're rushing your words or mumbling, this expresses your nervousness all the more. If you'll take a deep breath and slow down while enunciating, it will have a calming effect on your mind and your speech pattern. Assertive communication exudes self-control and voices words in a relaxed, respectful manner.

Now consider your dialogue. If it is full words like "uhhh" or "you know," you will seem as though you aren't speaking confidently or with much knowledge of the subject. Assertive communication doesn't use filler words; it uses direct, yet simple language such as "I feel" or "I want." Using shorter sentences communicates your desires more succinctly without giving in to the feeling that you must explain your every stance (refer to Assertive Right number 2 to help reaffirm this thinking).

It's also important to consider your tone. Passive communication can be whiny, conveying uncertainty or neediness. Aggressive communication can be gruff or sharp, conveying annoyance or anger. Assertive communication is neutral. You aren't asking permission, nor are you commanding with your tone. If you're trying to get your point across, again, think of how you would prefer to hear someone tell you what you want. It's likely that you'd prefer a respectful exchange like this: "I appreciate that you are working on another project right now. I could use your help on this question. Could we schedule 30 minutes this afternoon to discuss it?"

Now let's look at language—the specific words—that will help you articulate what exactly it is you want. There are four different techniques to employ verbal assertiveness. These statements, suggested by the University of Texas, can give you specific strategies for using your words to take a stance.

1. Basic assertion: Basic assertions are clear and straightforward statements of your wants, needs or beliefs. You say statements like, "I want to go out for dinner tonight," or "I need to attend to this matter, so can I call you back?" It's the most direct way to assert yourself.

A good place to use a basic assertion could be in response to a spouse asking, "What's for dinner tonight?" You could respond with, "I'd like to go try that new Chinese restaurant." The telephone is another place to use this as well. If someone calls you in the middle of a meal, you have every right to ignore the call. If you choose to answer, however, you can simply say, "I'm glad to hear from you, but I'm having dinner right now. May I call you back in a half hour?" This is respectful, but in basic terms, explains that you are meeting your own needs first.

2. Empathy. Empathy starts by expressing understanding for the other person. First, you recognize the other person's feelings or situation. Then you make a statement that asserts your rights, for example, "I realize you're busy, but I want us to succeed on this project. I need to meet with you today." The first statement gives full credence to the other person's plight. The second statement explains why you need their attention. The third statement gives specifics as to what you expect to happen.

You can use this technique to lead into a conversation that you realize may be confrontational. Or you can use it if you aren't comfortable starting with a basic assertion.

3. Escalate. Escalate means you become increasingly firm while remaining calm and in control. Perhaps the other person failed to respond to your assertion and continues to ignore your needs. At this point, you escalate the conversation. You express you have options and explain that if they don't meet your needs, you will engage those options. For example, "If you can't refund my money as your policy states, I will call the Better Business Bureau."

You'll want to use this type of assertion carefully. Use it when you feel that you've exhausted all other methods. At the very least, it should be employed when basic assertion and empathy fail. Also, when you escalate, remember to escalate only the conversation, not your tone or mood. You want to avoid becoming angry or aggressive.

4. "I" or "Me." This may be the most effective assertive method for dealing with negative situations. First, you identify what the other person has done, and then you explain what the problem is. Finally, you state what it is that you want or need to happen to resolve the situation. For example, "Jim, when you call me fat, it makes me feel unloved. If you are going to be in a relationship with me, I want you to use respectful words." The three parts to this method allow you to focus on your needs and the results you want, rather than on negative feelings.

You can also use "I" and "me" statements to prevent accusations or labels. If someone is acting rude, instead of telling them "You are rude," you can say "I feel like you are being rude." Or if you want to address a person's lack of attention, instead of saying "You don't listen," you can reply with "To me, it seems you don't listen." By saying "I feel" or "to me" you are not accusing the person, you are simply saying that's how it appears to you. This opens the conversation better without the other person feeling like he or she is being attacked.

Using "I" or "me" and simple statements can help you keep in control of your side of the conversation, and you can employ it almost any time you feel that the other person doesn't understand your meaning.

These are the methods of good, effective verbal communication. They should work in almost any situation in which you find yourself, from business settings to your personal life. The key is to remain calm and in control of your emotions and physical presence while focusing on being clear and concise with your words.

Practice

Before jumping into the above techniques of voice and physical demeanor in your everyday life, it is important to practice them first. Practicing can have a dramatic effect on your assertive performance. It can make the difference between good and great. Publilius Syrus once said "practice is the best of all instructors."

One easy way to practice assertiveness is with yourself. Under the section Walk the Walk, we talked about practicing eye contact in the mirror. You can use the mirror to practice other aspects of your body language as well. You can practice your smile, posture, and gestures. You can also practice the word and tone of your conversation. To go one step further, you can even rehearse potential scenarios, pretending your refection in the mirror is the person with whom you want to communicate. This will help you to adopt the new, assertive behavior more quickly.

Another way to practice is to ask your friends or family to role-play specific scenarios in which you want to be assertive. For example, if you want to learn to be more assertive with your boss, have your friend pretend to be your boss while you use the assertive language to explain why it won't be possible to work overtime this weekend. Then, reverse the roles. Imagine yourself being assertive from the boss's point of view. What insight do you gain by being in his shoes and how can you change your approach to be firm and clear, yet respectful in your resolve?

After the exercise, ask your friend how you performed. You'll gain valuable insight from a third person perspective. While you're listening to your friend's feedback, do so assertively. This means looking them in the eye and acknowledging their comments. Ask clarifying questions. Take notes if you like, but don't keep your eyes on the paper—maintain eye contact.

Finally, act! Don't procrastinate about this important new skill you're developing. It's like a muscle—the more you use it, the stronger and better defined it will be. Thomas Jefferson said, "Do you want to know who you are? Don't ask. Act! Action will delineate and define you." Get to know your true needs and wants better and then act assertively to make sure that everyone else knows them as well. Raise your hand in class, ask for help at work, look your friends in the eye, and tell them how much you appreciate their support.

All that you have learned up to this point are the fundamentals of good assertive communication. To summarize, begin with respect. You don't want to come across as overly aggressive or overly passive. Next, develop a healthy self-perception. If you lack self-esteem, you will exert tremendous effort selling your assertiveness. Furthermore, maintain confident body language and voice tone. People respond to you positively if they perceive you positively. A positive perception is communicated through positive body language. These are the keys of effective, assertive communication.

Like any form of communication, assertiveness is very context dependent. That is, how you approach an interaction will vary depending on where you are—at work, at home, or a restaurant—and who you are talking to—a boss, a co-worker, or a child. You don't want to interact with your boss the same way as you would a child, and you don't want to interact with a child the same way as you would a server at a restaurant. Different contexts require a different approach.

Given the intricate and wide-ranging variations in context, in the subsequent chapters, we will discuss common assertive situations in which you may find yourself. We will present examples and detailed instructions on how best to act and react in these situations. This will give you a better understanding of assertiveness. You will have a better look into how assertiveness works and where the commonalities and differences lie. Not all the scenarios may apply to you; nonetheless, go through them. Together, they paint a well-rounded and clear picture of how an assertive person acts. Let's move forward.

CHAPTER 3 - PUT YOUR PLAN TO WORK IN YOUR PERSONAL RELATIONSHIPS

You don't get harmony when everybody sings the same note.
—Doug Floyd

Ah, home sweet home. Home should be a place full of comforts where you can feel loved just for being you. Unfortunately, for many people who lack assertiveness, their relationships at home are just another word for "battleground." If you lack the boundaries to be heard and respected at home, you will feel as if you're always compromising your wants and needs in order to keep the peace in your relationships.

This is truly unfortunate as there are enough struggles with people in the outside world. If you want your relationships to be a haven, a safe respite from the storm, it is important to assert yourself with the people to whom you are close.

Whether it's a partner or spouse, child or parent, having boundaries for yourself and respecting others in your home can create that much-needed soft space on which to land at the end of a long day.

Your Heart, Your Reflection

We will start the discussion of relationships with significant others. It's been said that "We always hurt the ones we love the most." When someone loves you, there is an unwritten and unsaid rule that that person will be there for you and will take care of your needs. When your needs are not met, it is hurtful. Even though they love you, their love creates pain.

Many times this hurt results from miscommunication. Miscommunication causes pain when partners don't express their needs and wants clearly and with respect. Your partner may feel that he or she is doing all the right things to be a good spouse, but if you never communicate what was done wrong or what he or she should be doing right, that person will never know. Assertive, respectful communication prevents the hurtful situations caused by miscommunication and assures that each person has a chance to be heard, and more importantly, have his or her needs met.

You teach your partner how to treat you, and here's how to use assertive communication to teach that partner to treat you with love and respect.

1. Take Back the Power. At one point in your relationship, you made the decision to share a home with this person. If you feel that you can't be comfortable there, you can repeat the following: "No one has the right to make me feel uncomfortable in my own home." There. You've just set (or reset) the first basic paradigm for yourself.

2. Determine What You Want. Figure out what changes you desire in the relationship. If you don't know what you are seeking, how will your partner know? If you are not clearly expressing your needs and wants in a calm, assertive way (and preferably not in the middle of an argument), then part of the dilemma is stemming from you. Determine what it is that you crave from this person so you can clearly communicate it.

3. Communicate Your Want. Utilizing the physical and verbal assertiveness strategies discussed in Chapter 2, find time to discuss your relationship with your partner calmly. This doesn't need to be an over-dramatic "We need to talk" moment. Merely set aside some time to say, "I want our life together to continue and improve." Then explain what you want using "I" or "me" statements. Be willing to listen truly and actively to your partner's responses and needs as well. Being able to communicate your wants will help your partner appreciate your position in the relationship.

4. Continue to Be Caring. Asserting yourself with your spouse does not give you an excuse to become less giving or caring. Setting boundaries with your significant other means opening your heart so that you can better project and reflect love. It's vital to the growth of your relationship.

In fact, part of the boundaries you should be establishing should include setting specific time aside to spend in a low-pressure way with the person you love. Date night doesn't have to be fancy dinners out. It could be a quiet night at home or a relaxing walk together. Realize that you need to guard your time together and set that boundary to help your relationship flourish.

Now that you have a series of strategies to help you communicate with your partner, let's look at some scenarios that will show you how to put this information to use.

Scenario 1

Problem: You seem to fight all the time about household chores.

Suggestion: Sit down together and list out all the chores that require attention. Often we become so consumed with what we do for the other person that we forget the things the other person does for us. For instance, you may think that you are the only one who cleans and maintains the house. However, you may overlook all the work your spouse may be doing to maintain the yard, driveway, and garage as well as taking care of the major repairs when things go wrong. Writing the list gives you both a clear idea of how much each person contributes to the overall chores.

After creating the list, determine if the responsibilities are lopsided. You may find that your spouse is, in fact, very involved in many of the day-to-day activities. In that case, you may realize that you need to be the person lending the hand. On the opposite end, the list may confirm that household chores are lopsided against you, while your partner does little. In this case, discuss how the two of you will separate the duties more evenly. Discuss what chores you are willing to do and which chores you expect your partner to do. More importantly, discuss which chores you can do together or take turns doing.

This is a chance for open dialogue and compromise. It is not a time for you to begrudgingly accept the majority of the work just to keep the peace. You can utilize "I" and "me" statements or approach this with empathy. For example, you could begin with, "I know it isn't much fun doing housework, but it needs to be done. Someone has to do them, and that someone is us. I am willing to share this burden with you as we need to work as a team."

Once duties are separated, hold each other accountable for getting the work done. Make sure that your partner holds his/her end of the bargain. More importantly, make sure you hold your end as well. Otherwise you will seem hypocritical, causing your partner to mistrust you.

Scenario 2

Problem: You feel your partner doesn't listen to you.

Suggestion: Begin by assessing how you converse with your partner. When you talk to your partner, how do you speak? Do you always whine, moan and complain? Are you constantly harsh, vulgar and rowdy? If you are doing either, you are causing your own problems. Speaking to people in a whiny or harsh tone is draining. As mentioned in the last chapter, the wrong tone makes the other party stop paying attention. He or she may not even realize they are doing this, they simply begin to tune out.

If this is your normal mode of communication with your partner, it may be the reason your partner does not listen. He or she cannot help but tune you out. To prevent your partner from resisting your efforts to communicate, don't be overly harsh or loud. More importantly, don't let this be your baseline method of communication with your partner. Instead, talk to your significant other as though you are both adults. The person is not your parent that you run to with all your problems, and neither is that person a bratty child who requires reprimanding. This person is your significant other with whom you share your experiences.

Maybe the reason you started to whine and or sound harsh in the first place is because your partner never listens. That is, the problem is not in fact with you, but rather with your partner. If the problem is stemming from your partner, then this is the time to use assertive communication. When you confront your partner, look at each other. Be firm. Don't approach your partner whining or crying about how you feel. Don't demand your partner's attention, either. Use the specific language techniques explained in Chapter 2 and calmly assert, "When you don't pay attention to me, it makes me feel invisible. I have something important to discuss with you. Please turn off the TV so we can discuss it."

Also, be mindful of your partner's needs. Understand where your partner is coming from. Your partner may be preoccupied with work or have other things on his or her mind that is creating the distraction. If your partner is preoccupied with work or stressed about an upcoming event, be cognizant of this. He or she may need a listening ear first before shifting their focus to you. Remember, assertive communication is about the other person's perspective as well.

Scenario 3

Problem: You're not satisfied with your sex life.

Suggestion: Sex is vital to any relationship. In fact, many experts agree that sex is the glue that binds a healthy partnership. The problem is that sex can be complex. Not only is sex seen as taboo, but many times people feel awkward talking about it, especially with their partner.

If you feel uneasy about the topic, it's important to establish a level of trust and security with your partner to feel comfortable enough to express yourself. You can begin to build trust by talking about your likes outside of the bedroom rather than in the heat of the moment, which is likely to distract you both and may not result in a productive, respectful conversation. You may find your partner is willing to give more to you physically and emotionally in the bedroom if you are willing to communicate in a respectful way.

Another way to approach this is to actually take charge and assert your desires. Show your partner what you want. Some people would be relieved to have their partner show them rather than discuss it, so don't be afraid to "take charge." Remember, assertiveness comes with respect. This isn't an opportunity to suddenly become aggressive unless you've come to an agreement with your partner beforehand.

Often difficulty in asserting your sexual desires arise if you are uncomfortable with your physical appearance. If you are not comfortable enough with your body to feel safe with someone else, this can affect your intimate relationship. Feelings of shame or disappointment about your appearance may be projected to your partner. It can be hard for your partner to desire someone who doesn't like him or herself and therefore is noticeably uncomfortable with intimacy. If this is an issue for you, spend some time evaluating what you do like about your body. If you begin to think of your beautiful features, you may find ways to emphasize those features through your dress and demeanor.

Parenting Children

Being a parent can be one of the most simultaneously challenging and rewarding experiences in life. Good parents work hard to provide the best for their children so they can grow up to be successful, productive members of society.

In an effort to provide the best, however, parents sometimes fail to set proper boundaries. They fail to show their adolescents how to behave, how to treat others, as well as how to take care of things and clean up after themselves. More importantly, they may fail to set the correct limits as it relates to respect and courtesy for their parents. If you want your children to treat you with kind words instead of eye rolls, and respond to your requests rather than to ignore you, you need to apply a certain degree of assertiveness in your interactions with them.

As mentioned, assertiveness is about mutual respect. This applies to children as well. It is not about submitting to their every cry because they are so precious to you, and it is not about being overly authoritative in a way that implies your child needs you to supervise their every move. Communicating assertively with your child is about having a positive relationship where you are there for them and they are appreciative of your efforts and aware of their responsibilities. Speaking assertively with children conveys respect while simultaneously commanding respect.

To speak assertively with your children, use clear, concise statements like, "Please clean your room." You are not asking them, and neither are you yelling at them. You are conveying that they are worthy of your respect and you of theirs.

As always, stay away from aggressive and passive communication. Using aggressive or abusive language isn't likely to teach children how to treat others and will simultaneously lower their self-esteem. In fact, your tactic of aggressiveness may backfire, causing your child to resist you and your instructions even further. On the other hand, if you are passive and take a "hands off" approach, you will likely leave your children guessing as to what you expect of them and how they should respond to you. Even worse, a passive approach gives the impression that it is o.k. to continue to act inappropriately. Be firm, but not bossy.

Let's look at some examples of how you can be more assertive when interacting with your children. Say you want your child to become more involved with household chores as he/she gets older and asks for more privileges. An assertive parent could begin the conversation this way: "Lance, I know you have asked me to extend your curfew. I will consider doing this, but we need to discuss how you can do more around the house to help out first. I will need you to load and unload the dishwasher each day and I want you to start doing some of your own laundry. I will show you how to do this, but you will need to keep this up each week. If you can show responsibility in your chores, I will consider extending your curfew."

As another example, if your child tends to ignore you or your rules or constantly talks back to you, you could say: "Lee, I love you. However, the way you are treating me tells me that you are angry with me and is disrespectful. I want this to stop and I want us to get along better. When I ask you to do something, I want it done the first time without a sarcastic response. If you can't do this, I will take away your privileges to use the car or to play video games. I'd like to hear your thoughts on why our relationship has become so difficult and how you can help improve it."

In both of the above examples, your comments use clear, concise statements that communicate what you want. You are standing your ground without being pushy. You are giving your child respect, while setting specific rules and boundaries he or she craves. This shows that you are in charge of the situation and you will not tolerate bad behavior.

The above examples are generic scenarios, but the assertive pattern can be molded and applied to many types of situations you encounter with your child. Whatever the situation, what you want to do is:

• Express respect and love for your children.

• Tell them what is going wrong and why you're not happy with them.

- Tell them specifically what you expect them to do and how to treat you.

- Explain the consequences if they can't comply with your rules.

- Finally, actively listen to your children so they can explain their side. Then you can open the discussion up further to come to an agreement together.

The bottom line, dealing with your children assertively is the same as with any other person: When you treat someone with respect and are clear in your meaning, that person is more likely to respond with the same respect. This will take patience and time, but mostly it will take practice. Honest, open expression, however, is something you will probably find that your children will respond well to and could enhance your relationship dramatically.

Reversing Roles

Now that we have discussed how to be assertive with children, let's swing to the other end and talk about how to apply assertiveness when dealing with parents. Obviously, if you have a positive and healthy relationship with your parents, there is no need to assert yourself with them; however, if you have overbearing, judgmental, or otherwise difficult parents and it is affecting the quality of your life, it is important to stand up and break their incessant behavior.

Overbearing or judgmental parents may believe that it is not only their right, but their duty to speak to their adult children in a way that is construed as less than respectful. They may criticize where you live, your career path, or even the partner you have chosen. The way you raise your own children may even become a contentious topic.

To handle difficult parents, it helps to first examine your relationship with them. Are you always seeking their approval or constantly acting needy? Are you irresponsible? If so, you are setting your own limits in how they treat you. If you are always trying to gain the approval of your parents and run to them when you have a problem rather than trying to face it on your own, they will see you as a child. As a result, they will treat you like one.

If you want them to show you respect, look at your actions that externally project your status as a child and change them. Let go of always trying to get their approval. Stop acting needy and take charge of yourself and your life. If you make mistakes, acknowledge them and take the appropriate actions to find a solution. Don't always look to them for the solution. The more you act like a mature adult, the more people will treat you like one, including your parents.

The expectation is not that you become fully independent from your parents. There will come times when you will need their support. If what you're really after is a lending hand and a listening ear, then let them know that. You can preface your conversation with: "I'm mulling something over and would like your opinion." When they offer their opinion, you can respectfully say, "Thanks for listening. I will consider what you've said, but will be making my own decision later."

Becoming your parents' ally and friend rather than just their child can have long-lasting benefits for both of you. Your parents will likely feel less of a self-imposed responsibility to continually parent you. Simultaneously, you are less likely to feel a similar self-imposed responsibility to live up to their expectations. You may find that you actually enjoy being your parents' friend more than you enjoyed being their child.

If the difficulty in interacting with your parents is not a result of any childish behavior on your end, then the issue is your parents. If your parents are holding you back from leading a mature and independent life, it is time to set boundaries. Look at what you might have done as an adult that gave them the idea that they could treat you disrespectfully. Then use what you have learned in this book to set those boundaries with them.

If indeed, you have tried to establish boundaries that your parents refuse to respect, you must lay some ground rules for yourself and for them. For example, your mother comes over to your house for dinner and complains the entire time she's there about your home and the meal you've made. You can reply with, "Mom, I invited you over here tonight because I love you and wanted to spend some time together. This is my home that I have chosen and I pay for it myself. I no longer live in your home. When you criticize my home and the meal I've served, you are insulting me. I want us to work together to change that so we can treat each other with respect. You are welcome here, but only if you can speak to me respectfully."

This may seem extreme or harsh, but when you establish that your home is yours, not hers, and the behavior you expect from her while she is in your home, you lay the boundary lines. If your mother chooses to continue to belittle you while in your home, she now knows that she is crossing those lines and will no longer be welcome there.

The older we get, the more set we get in our ways, and the harder it is to change. This means the more you're going to have to stand your ground. If your mother has been mistreating for a long time, it will not be easy for her to change that habit. She may frown, pucker, resist and pout. You may have to endure the silent treatment from her. You could offer to try a visit in her home, but with the understanding that you will only do so if she can speak respectfully to you.

Parents who refuse to treat their adult children as peers can be a complex, difficult situation, but if you approach the topic with respect and calm, clear directives about how you want to be treated, you can begin to change the dynamics of the relationship. Aggressive behavior from parents is like aggressive behavior from anyone else. It's best met with respectful, clear assertions of what you want and need and what is not acceptable behavior in the relationship.

Parenting Your Parents

If, someday, you find that the parent/child relationship roles are reversed and that you need to care for your parents, having a relationship based on mutual regard can make this transition easier. As adults, we are sometimes called upon to become a caretaker for a parent. Whether this is due to injury or illness or for financial reasons, shifting from being your parent's child and (hopefully) friend to their advocate and caretaker can be extremely difficult. It becomes more difficult if the parent has health issues that affect memory or behavior, such as dementia or Alzheimer's disease.

48

If you find yourself in this situation, it becomes critical that you set boundaries for both you and your parent. Sadly, you may feel as though you have become the parent and the parent is now the child—hence the subtitle of Parenting Your Parents. Just as your parents cared for you, it's now your job to care for them. Being an assertive communicator will give you some useful tools in working with others to ensure that your parent is receiving what he or she needs.

First, realize that it may not be possible for you to do everything. It may be physically impossible for you to work full time, raise your own children, and care for your parent each and every day. Assertive communication allows you to step off the "merry-go-round" for a moment and say, "I need help." There should be no shame or regret in saying this. In fact, the more that you can admit this fact to yourself, the more empowered you will be to delegate tasks so that your parent receives the best possible care.

If you have siblings, this is the time to use assertive communication with "I need" and "I want" statements that explain how you'd like to create a plan for your parent's care. For example, you can say, "Hailey, I need a break today so that I can take care of some errands. Would you please check on Mom at 12:00 to make sure she eats lunch? I am going to spend some time with her tonight, so I have to take care of these errands." This is clear and respectful communication that gives you some breathing room, as well.

If your parent is in a hospital, you can use assertive communication to become his or her best advocate. It may feel awkward at first, but if you ask questions, the more likely you are to understand what is being done to care for your parent. For example you might say, "Dr. Smith, I'm not sure I understand why you've changed Dad's medication. He seems to be feeling worse now. Could you please explain the new course of treatment to me?" Your question may clear up some concerns you or your Dad have about how he's feeling since starting the new medication. Your Dad may have been feeling too sick to ask the question himself.

When speaking with your parent, utilizing "I" statements and empathy are likely to help you assert yourself. For example, "Mom, I know you aren't feeling well today. I'm here to help you. But when you yell at me and call me incompetent, it hurts my feelings. Please be more respectful as I'm trying to help you get better." If you were to merely suffer your mom's verbal abuse in silence, it's not likely that you would be able to care for her for very long, and your feelings of aggression would likely fester.

Taking on the care of a sick parent can be overwhelming, but there are a myriad of resources available to those who need help. Don't be afraid to talk to your parent's doctor for suggestions as to outside sources that can provide for your parent's needs. Again, admitting that your mental and physical resources aren't boundless can be difficult, but if you allow yourself to set clear boundaries as to what you can and cannot provide for your parent and convey that information respectfully to everyone involved, this process will become easier each day. You'll give yourself the breathing room you need to plan and execute their care.

Now that you're communicating assertively in your personal life, it's time to examine how you can best use these strategies in your professional life.

CHAPTER 4 - MAKING
IT WORK (AT WORK)

Too many of us fail to fulfill our needs
because we say no rather than yes, yes when
we should say no
.—William Glasser

There are many complex interactions that take place every day in business. Perhaps the most important one occurs when you assertively communicate what you want to the people who can make it happen. To ensure you receive the best results, you must employ your best tactics. Of course, the best communication tactic is assertive.

When you offer your "A Game" of assertive communication skills, you ensure that your needs and wants are clearly expressed, that no one feels disrespected by your request, and that you've set boundaries as to timelines, deadlines, and what you're willing to accept and do to complete a task.

Utilizing assertiveness doesn't guarantee you will be granted your every request, especially in the workplace; however, by using assertiveness, you ensure that you've put forth your best effort to present your information and request in a clear, respectful way.

Dealing with Difficult Co-workers

As in the previous chapter, let's look at a couple of examples of how assertiveness can help you at work.

Scenario 1

Problem: Your co-worker for an important project has been recently slacking off and has asked you to cover for him at a meeting next week. You want to say "no," but you want to do so without creating tension.

Suggestion: Set up a convenient time to talk for both of you to open communication with respect. Once you're meeting with your co-worker, the conversation could go like this: "Tom, I understand that you've had some difficulty with the project. However, I am not only juggling this project, but another that has a tight deadline. While I appreciate the work you have contributed, I am not able to complete the project for you. I will present my work at the meeting next week. I want you to present your own work. I believe if you put forth the same effort you initially exerted to complete this project, we'll have a great meeting."

At no point are you disrespectful of Tom's feelings; in fact, you've complimented him. Your assertiveness, however, has allowed you to tell Tom, "These are my boundaries. No, I will not cover for you. I expect you to do your best work." Assertiveness has allowed you to keep your dignity, respect Tom's feelings and clearly set boundaries by explaining to him that you don't accept the way he is trying to treat you.

It may not always be possible to set up a meeting; an immediate answer may be necessary when someone is trying to push you to give them an answer. In these cases, you can still act. To do so, stop what you're doing, look Tom in the eye and say, "Tom, I'm not going to be able to fit your project into my schedule. I think you're the best person to present this work at the meeting." If you've been direct, clear and respectful in your tone with Tom, he will understand the message and you'll have shut down his persistent requests assertively.

Scenario 2

Problem: Debbie, a coworker, talks about you behind your back constantly, interrupts your presentations with inane questions and tries to make you feel uncomfortable every time you are around her. You want to stop Debbie's rude behavior.

Suggestion: Unfortunately, aggression, bullying and outright rude behavior aren't limited to the schoolyard. You may encounter colleagues or bosses who treat you with little to no respect. This is a perfect time for you to utilize assertive communication tactics to stop this unacceptable behavior.

Your approach should be direct, reserved and crystal clear in its meaning. You should not confront Debbie in front of others, but find a moment when you can talk to her alone, perhaps in an otherwise empty conference room.

The conversation could go like this: "Debbie, you seem to have a problem with me. We don't have to be personal friends, but we do have to work together. When you are openly hostile toward me, it is disrespectful and makes me feel negative about working together. As your colleague, I deserve your respect. I would like to improve our communication. I want you to know that I will no longer accept your aggressive attitude toward me. If it doesn't cease, I'll be setting up a meeting for us with Human Resources to discuss it further. I would appreciate it if you would consider how you speak to me and treat me with more respect."

Debbie is likely to be flabbergasted by the fact that you've calmly and assertively called her bluff. If indeed, she does not back down and proceeds to become more aggressive or threatens to cause more trouble for you in your job, you should thank her for her time, turn on your heel and immediately go to HR to file a complaint. You defined your boundaries, and you may have to move forward with actions (going to HR) to defend them.

Scenario 3

Problem: You have a rude and pushy boss and you want to stand up against his or her disrespectful behavior.

Suggestion: We'll offer a suggestion by starting with a great tale of assertiveness in the workplace. A young laboratory assistant made an error in her work in the laboratory. While the error didn't pose any danger or harm to anyone, it did cause a delay in the timeline of the experiment her boss was performing. When the employee returned from lunch, her boss screamed at her about the error in front of their colleagues and told her she was "better than this." Fighting tears of embarrassment, the employee retreated to the bathroom and had a good cry. When she returned to the laboratory, she silently cleaned up the lab ware for the experiment to begin again. She said nothing to her boss for the rest of the day.

The next morning, she knocked on her boss's office door and asked if he had a moment. Closing the door behind her, the young employee sat down across from her boss and looked him squarely in the eye. Then she apologized for the error. Next, she calmly told him that he humiliated her in front of the entire lab. She reminded him that she was his subordinate, but that she was also his colleague, and that he had treated her disrespectfully.

She followed that by saying she would make every effort not to make the same mistake, and that she expected him not to ever make the same mistake of forgetting that she was his colleague. She concluded by telling him if he treated her that way again, she would file a formal complaint with the head of the laboratory for verbal abuse. Her boss apologized. The employee continued to work with him for another 2 years before she left for another job, and they never had another conflict.

There were a few things that came together for this young woman to diffuse this overly aggressive conflict. First, instead of reacting immediately with fear or anger, she took some time to collect her thoughts. Second, she respectfully requested her boss's time the next morning and sat down and looked him in the eye, which told him with her body language that she wasn't intimidated by him. Third, she used "I" and "me" language to express how she felt. Finally, she emphasized the seriousness of the event by using escalating

CHAPTER 4 - MAKING IT WORK (AT WORK)

language: telling her boss that if he couldn't treat her with respect, she would file a formal complaint.

The reason he may have felt that it was his right to talk to her so aggressively was because he was her boss. He mistakenly believed that treating a subordinate badly was acceptable behavior until she reminded him that as a colleague, they were equals under the rules of their workplace. Had she believed him and remained a passive, subordinate employee, they would have never gained one another's understanding and mutual regard.

Additionally, while it would have been very easy to have cried or even screamed back at her boss that day, neither of those actions would have gained his understanding of her boundaries. When faced with a conflict at work, if your communication style is to get angry or whine about your situation, you're not likely to gain the respect of anyone, including yourself. Assertive communication allows you the opportunity to set the necessary boundaries to deal with conflicts and daily challenges as they arise.

An important distinction needs to be made in this woman's use of escalating language. If you notice, she utilizes escalating language the first time she confronts her boss. She tells her boss that if he treats her that way again, she would file a formal complaint. You don't necessarily have to use escalating language so quickly.

Escalating language can be reserved for when you need to "escalate" your assertiveness. The technique can be applied in response to the other person ignoring or neglecting your initial attempt at being assertive. In other words, if her boss disregarded her original request and continued to disrespect her, she could come back in her second meeting to make use of the escalating language. So if you are nervous about escalating language, you can refrain from using it until it becomes necessary.

The wonderful thing about assertive communication is that you don't have to worry about changing your behavior between a superior or a subordinate because the underlying message is one of respect. Respect was discussed in the introduction as being the defining difference between assertiveness and aggression. When you speak with assertive language, you take the other person's feelings, opinions, and time into respectful consideration, regardless of his or her title, position or salary level within the organization.

Thus your conversation with your boss may be more formal, but it would carry the same tone and words of respect that you would use when talking to your peer about the same issue. You would ensure that both the CEO and assistant had the time to discuss the problem; you would explain what they've done and what your boundaries are, and you would give them your full physical attention (eye contact, facing them) as you listened to their questions.

Not only will assertive communication help you clearly tell others what you want and need, it will save you time from having to figure out how to talk to different people in different positions of authority in the company—whether they are a superior or subordinate. The answer is simple: Each person is deserving of the respect inherent in assertive communication.

How to Assertively Ask for a Raise

Now that you have an understanding of how you can use assertiveness in the workplace, let's use it in another work-related situation everyone at some point finds himself or herself in—asking for a raise.

Of all the possible work encounters, asking for a raise can be the most intimidating. Almost everyone is nervous and unsure about how to approach the boss in this situation. Should you act humble or toot your own horn? Should you make an appointment with the boss or just try to corner him in a social atmosphere and send some hints? The problem is that you know that if you say nothing, nothing is probably what you will get.

Your best strategy for approaching this situation is to plan, prepare, and present your case. You may want a raise and need it even more, but getting ahead of yourself can cause setbacks and problems. It's best to be methodical in your approach and clear and respectful in your discussion.

Here are some guidelines for handling this sticky situation. Each boss or supervisor is different and may require some adjustments.

First, make an appointment with your boss to discuss this issue. Inform him or her of what you'd like to discuss beforehand. This is respectful of his/her time and will give both of you an opportunity to prepare for the meeting.

Next, do your homework. Gather evidence as to why you deserve the raise. Look at salaries for people with your level of skills and experience, which are readily available through internet searches. Consider other additional training you've received, successful projects, awards, accolades from colleagues, customer reviews, sales numbers, etc. In addition, make a list of your relevant skills—those which have made you or make you successful in your job.

Finally, when you have the meeting, use your assertive skills. Start with your body language. Walk in tall. Say hello. Shake his or her hand. Sit down and look him or her in the eye.

Then utilize assertive language to express your desire for the raise. Begin by saying: "Joni, I've asked to meet with you today about my salary. I appreciate your time. I would like to receive an increase of x percent and have some reasons to explain why I believe I am deserving of it."

At this time, discuss your reasons—"I've never been late to work." "I finish all my tasks on time." "I take initiative when necessary." Present your research. You can also mention what additional work you are willing to take on. "I am willing to do a, b and c in my job if I receive this raise. I'd like to hear your thoughts."

This is your opening. It's the beginning of your dialogue. You've been respectful, completely clear, and you've set boundaries for what you are willing to do to receive the pay increase. In other words, you've just assertively asked for a raise.

If you have successfully presented your argument, your boss ought to agree to the raise. More than likely, he will need time to think it over. As a result, do not pressure your boss to give you an answer right away. He or she may be busy and have a lot on his plate that needs attention. If so, let him or her take care of those issues.

Also, your boss may need to perform due diligence to see if a raise is in the budget and/or discuss it with his or her manager before making any decisions. Even your boss has to be accountable to higher-ups, so you may need to continue the discussion in subsequent meetings. If another meeting is required, be prepared with additional points in case he or she decides to argue against the raise.

If your boss does argue against it, whether in the initial meeting or after having a chance to mull it over, listen carefully to what he or she has to say. Even if the answer to your request ends up being "no," that does not mean it is the end of it. Be a good listener and ask why you did not qualify for the raise. When you ask, be polite. Getting angry and demanding for concrete answers will not help you at all.

Take a deep breath and calmly present your counter argument. If your boss says you don't have the skills, present examples that illustrate how you do have them or make it clear that you are willing to learn. If the argument is that there are others more qualified, explain where your skill sets exceed theirs. Your counter argument is important because even if your boss feels you are deserving of a raise and has the ability to give it to you, many times he or she will still deny your initial request. That is part of being a good manager. They are not going to hand out a raise to every employee that walks in and asks for one.

If after presenting your counter argument, your boss is still insistent, then you know he or she is not saying no for the sake of saying no. Therefore, this person may have legitimate reasons as to why he or she can't give you the raise. Ask your boss what you can do to increase your chances. Find out how you can improve your performance.

Take to heart what your boss tells you about improving your performance and put it into practice as soon as possible. Be willing to do what is necessary (within reason, that is) to ensure that the next time you ask for a raise, you will receive a favorable reply. Your willingness to improve weighs in your favor. In the meantime continue to perform at work.

There is a good possibility that if your boss does agree to a raise, it will be for a date in the near future. He or she will want to wait anywhere from a one to six months for the raise to start. Consider this a win. Your boss is doing this because he wants to make sure that you will stay committed to your word. The time he has you wait will be a test of your commitment. During this transitory period, make sure to continue to perform. You don't want him or her to re-consider this generosity.

If your boss does agree to a raise, there is also a good possibility that he or she will not give you the exact amount you asked. The raise offered might be for a lesser amount. In this case, you will have to decide whether the increase, albeit smaller, is still a win. If the offer is more than half of what you asked, it's likely a favorable response. Conversely, if the offer is less than half, it is likely not a win and you are being offered just enough to keep you off his back. If you find the lower offer to be satisfactory, thank him respectfully. If not, handle it as you would handle a denial; ask what you can do to get the increase you initially set forth or counter with reasons why you feel you deserve more.

Unfortunately, you might be in a situation where you have a boss who, pardon my French, is simply a "prick." Even though you are deserving of a raise, he won't give you one. He may even lead you to believe that a potential raise or promotion is in sight, but not keep his word. Worse, he may offer the raise or promotion to a lesser qualified and/or experienced staff member. This is the fact of life. Businesses are riddled with superiors and managers whose treatment of employees is not based on merit, rather personal preference.

In this situation, you want to take a good hard look and determine if that company is right for you. If your boss ignores your efforts and is getting in the way of your professional growth, then it may be time to move forward and look elsewhere for employment. This is part of the assertive process. If your needs are not being met or your rights are being violated, it is important to remove yourself from the "situation" and put yourself in a better situation. The situation in this case is a new place of employment.

Leaving your employer, however, is not always easy, especially in our current economy. For certain professionals, such as pilots or talent agents, moving to another company means giving up the seniority you have gained and starting back at the bottom. These are tough decisions to make; however, if you truly feel confident in your work and certain in your dedication as an employee, then a new job is an option worth considering. Just make sure to do your due diligence so you are not walking into the same situation with a new employer.

Before moving on, you might first try escalating language. If you are confident in a decision to find another job, you might let your boss know. If your boss insists on not giving you the raise you desire, let him know that you will consider going to another firm or company. When telling your boss this, try not to sound like you are making a threat or forcing him into a decision. Simply state it as an option you are willing to consider. In addition, don't bring it up early in the conversation. This is escalating language, remember, so bring it up when you have exhausted other avenues.

If you plan on escalating the discussion, make sure you are confident in your decision. Your boss may well let you leave. In this case, you are made aware sooner rather than later as to where you stand in his eyes, and it is best to move on to a place where you will be valued. Don't be angry or tempted to gripe excessively. Assertiveness does not mean that you always get your way, but rather it is about trying your best to stand up for your rights. If your best is not good enough for the current situation, move to one where it is. Put the past behind you and focus your energy on improving your future.

Lastly, if your boss does not come back to you with a response, ask when you might know. Don't leave empty-handed with an open-ended date. Take initiative to schedule the next meeting. It will be one step closer to getting a response.

These are the different ways to assertive yourself in the workplace. I realize the instructions presented here are pretty formal and structured, but that is because most work settings require a formal approach. Though depending on the culture and environment at your job, your approach might be more relaxed. Instead of setting up a meeting, you might just knock on your boss's door or walk up to your co-worker to ask if he or she has a second to talk. If the answer is "yes," bring up your concern. You don't have to be overly serious, but still be firm.

Learning to be assertive at work will earn you respect from your peers and your bosses. Being assertive means speaking up for yourself, handling conflicts, and getting problems solved. If you'd like to learn more ways to do that at work, remember to visit ScaredCocoon.com/free to download the bonus guide *Assertive at Work: Thriving in a Workplace of Mind Games and Bullies*. It's free and provides valuable insight into improving your strength and confidence in the workplace.

CHAPTER 5 - THE GLOBAL SHIFT FROM GOODS TO SERVICES

Only those who dare to fail greatly can ever achieve greatly. - Robert Kennedy

One real world application where you can easily begin to utilize your new assertive communication style is as a consumer. As a consumer, you may encounter situations where you don't feel in control of the purchasing process. You may feel pressure by a pushy salesperson to buy something you don't really want, or you may encounter a problem with a product you bought and feel serious buyer's remorse. Assertive communication can help you in both instances, and we'll discuss them in this chapter.

Not so long ago, customer service was considered an afterthought for many companies. They offered a product, but may not have really cared very much about a shopper's experience as he or she bought it or what happened after the purchase if there was a problem. Today, consumers have many factors in their favor to help them as they shop and make purchases.

First, retailers now want more than just your money. They want your loyalty. They want to make sure you continue to shop with them. As a result, they have put numerous systems in place should you have a problem with a product. You as a consumer have money-back guarantees, warranties, price-matching, no-questions asked returns and free return shipping as some of the safety nets behind your purchase. Retailers have a vested interest in your satisfaction to ensure you stay loyal.

Furthermore, the world economy has changed the way customers purchase products. This shift has made companies realize that they must offer more than just goods to the global marketplace. They must also offer customer service to attract and retain their consumer base. It is not enough for businesses to offer feature rich products: they need to provide excellent customer service as well.

More importantly, the internet has changed the playing field. It has made the market place more competitive, allowing consumers to be more informed shoppers and giving them more opportunities to broadcast their opinions about faulty products and services. Less than twenty years ago, if you wanted to buy something, you went to a store in your local area and purchased it. If the store did not have the item you wanted, there was not much you could do. To find out if a product was safe and reliable, you were limited to your circle of family and friends for a critique.

Now, if you want to purchase something, anything really, your options are wide open. You can go to a small specialty shop, a large department store, or online. If you want the product used, your options are even greater. You can do an internet search for it at home, or perhaps even better, stand in front of the product at the store, scan the package barcode with your smartphone and see available pricing in and around your area. Beyond that, now you can thoroughly research your product by reading professional critics' reviews from online magazines and journals or customer reviews, often from store websites, internet retailers, or the product's brand website. The internet has really expanded the horizon for consumers.

All of these fast-paced changes mean that there has never been a better time to be a consumer. However, you need to understand how best to deal with pushy salespeople or to negotiate pricing. After making a purchase, you'll need to know how to deal with a company's customer service department. Fortunately for you, you have the tool of assertiveness in your arsenal. Not so long ago, consumers' options were limited. Now they can do much more.

How to be an Assertive Buyer

Even though a consumer's options are more open, making a purchase, especially a large one, can still be unpleasant. Depending on what you are buying and from where, you may encounter rude or difficult sales staff that neglect your needs or push you into a buying decision. This can lead you to purchase the wrong item while paying too much for it. As a buyer, assertive communication when making a purchase allows you to set boundaries for yourself so that you don't feel pressure to:

• make an immediate purchase

• purchase something you don't want, or

• spend more money than you planned to.

As in other areas we've discussed, an assertive consumer is neither passive nor overly aggressive. Passive consumers tend not to really know what they need or want and may not communicate effectively. This leaves the company representative guessing as to what he or she can do to help, which may mean that the company does nothing. Aggressive customers go in knowing what they want and need, but are willing to step on whomever they need to get it, which usually leads to long, painful discussions with customer service representatives who would be well within their rights to deny assistance after being verbally abused.

An assertive consumer respectfully communicates what he or she needs and wants. This person is actually a "dream customer" for companies, which makes them eager to work with you to provide what you're asking for. To take the assertive route, here are some tips to communicate your needs and wants respectfully to feel more in control of the buying process.

1. Research the product you are looking to purchase. An educated customer is an empowered customer. When you research, you will have an idea of what is out there for the specific product or service. Your research will clue you into the different manufacturers, the prices retailers are asking, as well as the options that are available. By doing your research, you may uncover aspects of which you weren't previously aware about a product or service, but will influence your decision making.

You can go about your research a few different ways. You can begin by going online. If you can't find what you need from the internet, develop a list of questions that you can take to the store that sells the product to ask their salesperson. You can also research the brand's or store's competitors to get more information. The more information you have, the better.

2. Determine what you need. After you do your research, you will be in a better position to discern your needs. You will have a handy awareness of the types of products and options that exist and how they can benefit you. Figure out what options you require as well as the price you are willing and able to pay. You may be able to limit your search down to two or three products based on your "must have" list and budget. You can consider these limits as non-negotiable as you pursue your purchase.

3. Determine what you want. You can consider this your "wish list" of features that you'd like to have in the product or service, but are not a deal breaker if you don't get them. Your needs are not negotiable, but your wants can change based on the price and terms offered. Take your wants and needs list with you as you shop so that you're prepared to communicate with salespeople to remind them of what is and isn't negotiable as you move toward your purchase.

4. Use your brand loyalty as an asset. Many companies offer reward programs that give customers discounts, free items or even special financing. You can get everything from free flights or hotel nights to special sales that aren't available to the public by using loyalty programs wisely. Another area some customers overlook is their credit cards' loyalty programs. Many offer discounted shopping sites online allowing you to use your points to pay for items, or they offer a cash back program that equals money in your pocket. Some credit cards even offer to extend the warranty on purchases beyond the original manufacturer's warranty if you paid for the item with that card.

5. Ask. Ask. Ask. If you don't ask specifically for what you need and want, you're not likely to get it. If you want a red dress, but see a style you like only in gray, ask if it's available in red. It's especially important to focus on the tone of your voice to ensure that you don't sound whiny or angry, especially if you are speaking to someone on the phone. One crucial step for assertively communicating on the telephone is always to ask for the representative's name (and extension number, if possible). If your needs and wants are not being met with "We can't do that" from a representative, "ask" what the company can do for you.

6. It is o.k. to say no. If you are not interested in making a purchase at the moment or at all, you do not have to. Sometimes you may feel obligated to make a purchase if a sales person was nice enough to take care and spend time with you; however, remember from the Rights of Assertiveness, although you may feel concern and compassion and good will for others, you are not responsible for their happiness. If a salesperson has been helpful, that is their job. That is what they get paid to do.

Additionally, many salespeople, especially really good ones, use this indebtedness people feel to guilt them into making a purchase decision they don't want. Often, the sales associate will pretend that he or she is your best friend, so you feel even more indebted to them. More often than not, these are well-known tactics used by well-trained sales people. You don't have to fall for their manipulation; you have every right to walk away from a purchase decision without feeling bad about it.

7. The power is on your side. As a purchaser, all the power is on your side. This is the most important tip. You are the one holding the money. Until you make a payment or sign a contract, you have the upper hand. If you don't like the terms of the purchase, you can simply take your business elsewhere.

A helpful trick to keep a seller from pressuring you to relinquish this power is to leave your wallet or purse in the car or at home when you go shopping. That is, if you feel walking into a store that you may not have the self-control to say "no" to a pushy salesperson, go in without any form of payment. This way, you can't be pushed into making a purchase because you have nothing on you with which to pay. If you do decide the purchase is right, you can walk out to your car or back home to get the money. While walking out, reflect on the decision to make sure you are not jumping the gun. If you decide that you are in fact jumping the gun in making the purchase, you don't have to go back in. You can simply drive away to the next store or seller, or even back home to mull things over.

Above are some tips to keep the power on your side as a consumer. Let's look at an example of how you can use these tips the next time you make a purchase. Let's say that you are in the market for a new car. Before going into any random dealership, do some research. Learn about the different types of cars such as SUVs, Sedans, Mini-Vans, and/or Crossovers that are out there. Take note of the relative price range you can expect to pay for each variety. In addition, find out the various options that are available within each class. Furthermore, research the numerous companies that manufacture these cars to determine their reliability.

Once you've done your research and are aware of what is out there, narrow in on your needs and wants. You may find that your needs include a car large enough to fit everyone in your family, but with a price tag that does not exceed $29,000. Moreover, you live in Chicago where it snows a lot, so you need a car that is either 4-wheel or All-wheel drive. Conversely, options like a sun roof and heated seats are things you want, but do not necessarily need. They may help to sweeten the deal, but you can do without.

After you determine what you need and want and have a price range in mind, pick out a few dealers in the area that sell that particular brand and model. Go in and talk to them about the car (but remember not to bring your wallet or purse in with you). You should go to the dealers armed with the following:

- A printout from a reputable website such as Edmunds.com showing the dealer's average cost for your car so that you can make a fair offer ($1,000 over dealer's invoice is generally considered a fair offer, but may vary with the market and car type).

- A specific list of the features you want, from engine size all the way down to paint and interior colors and the type of wheels you like.

- Your financing options. You should know your credit score and find out what finance rates you can get through your own bank before you explore financing the car through the dealer. If you are paying cash, you will have an additional bargaining chip on your side.

With the following tools, you can then begin to negotiate the purchase of your new car. The conversation might go like this: "James, I'm interested in this Jeep Cherokee and would like to discuss what your company can offer me in terms of features and pricing." Once James has made you an offer, if it isn't what you want, you could say, "I know that your dealership has paid around $27,000 for the car, and I'm willing to offer you $28,500 if you are willing to waive the delivery fees."

Once James has had a chance to respond, you can continue to assert yourself on other matters by saying, "I have my credit score, which is excellent. I've also checked with my bank, and they're offering a very competitive financing rate. If you would like my business, is your company willing to match that rate?" You could also ask the dealer to include items such as an extended warranty, complimentary maintenance, or add-ons such as dealer-installed features to sweeten their deal. As an assertive buyer, you hold the power to ask for what you want respectfully and see how the seller responds.

Realize you will not always be able to get everything you ask for. Often, a company will genuinely be unable to fulfill your request. For example, many car manufacturers do not offer luxury options like leather or heated seats in their lower end, less expensive models. It doesn't mean that they are trying to manipulate or take advantage of you. It simply means that they truly don't have that feature or service available. Not only are they unable to offer it to you, they are unable to offer it to anyone else. As a result, you may need to reassess your needs and wants.

Also realize that your needs and wants ought to be reasonable. If your maximum budget for a new car is $29,000, asking for a 7 series BMW at that price is unreasonable. The greatest assertiveness skills will not make that happen. Being an assertive buyer means getting what you want without being taken advantage of. It doesn't mean getting what you want to the extent that you take advantage of the seller. Sellers are in the business to make money, not to hand out charity to the most demanding individual.

Nonetheless, you should not allow yourself to feel pressured by a salesperson or representative to make a purchase or accept an offer that you're not comfortable with. If your needs aren't being met or if the sales process is moving too fast for your comfort, remember that an assertive consumer always retains the right to say "no." You don't need to apologize for that or feel that you're disappointing someone or that you're going to miss out on something if you're just not ready to make a purchase. Say, "No thank you," and move on to the next dealer on your list.

You can apply the above techniques with any buying decision, no matter how big or small. Do your research, find out what is available, determine what is negotiable and what is not, be firm, yet polite, and be willing to walk away.

Communicating Assertively When Product/Service Does Not Work

O.k., so you made a purchase. You used your new-found skills to buy exactly what you wanted at the price you wanted it. Everything was going great, but then six months into using the product or service, you began experiencing issues.

When a product or service does not work or stops working as promised, you don't have to accept it as your loss. You as a consumer have rights that protect you. However, you will have to employ some assertiveness to uphold those rights. Communicating assertively when something has gone wrong can help an otherwise difficult and frustrating situation be one where you feel in control and can calmly tell the company how to resolve your problem.

Here are some general tips when dealing with a company after you've made a purchase and start having problems with their product:

1. Understand the malfunction. First and foremost, determine the problem or malfunction. If something is not working, it is important to understand what that is: Does the device not power on? Is there a glitch in the software? Are the buttons not functioning, or do the menus not respond as intended? If you can figure out the exact issue, it will help you out. The more information you can provide, the better the company can assist you.

2. Gather your documents. Purchase documents are important in dealing with a claim. Everything from receipts to warranty certificates to an offer the company makes to resolve your problem is important. Don't rely on the company to have all your purchase information on file.

3. Ask for the next level of appeal. If the person you are dealing with (either on the telephone or in person) isn't willing to work with you to meet your needs and wants, you can ask to speak to the next level of appeal. Many people make the mistake of immediately demanding a supervisor who is over the whole department, but in doing so, may remove a few layers of opportunity for the company to satisfy your request. It can be difficult to have to repeat your story, but patience and persistence can be your allies in this case.

4. Keep climbing. If indeed the company still hasn't resolved your problem after another level or three of appeals, don't give up. You can get information about nearly anyone in the company, all the way up to the CEO or owner. Using your documentation skills as mentioned in tip number 6, write a certified letter or send an e-mail to the appropriate person in charge. You can set your email to send a receipt so that you'll know it was received and read. Then, follow up a day after you receive notice that your email or letter has been received. This step may seem extreme, but if your problem is an expensive fix, this step can be crucial for a resolution.

5. Always be respectful. You may be exasperated by talking to so many people, but don't allow your frustration to turn into disrespect. The person on the other end of the phone is in a position to help you and doesn't deserve the brunt of your anger. It's perfectly ok to say, "I'm really frustrated by this situation. Is there something you can do to help me?" This is honest, yet respectful.

6. Never say die. Be firm, be polite, and be clear and unrelenting. This does not mean that you should call the company every hour until they resolve your problem. You can call once a day or once a week to check on a larger problem if appropriate. Just as you have the right to say "no," remember that you also have the right not to accept "no" from the company. You may not get exactly what you were after, but compromise may be attainable, and that's probably more than you had to begin with. You also have alternatives outside of the company. Advocacy groups such as the Better Business Bureau exist for the exact purpose of helping customers and businesses resolve problems.

7. Keep detailed records. Records can be crucial to helping you document the process of dealing with a company. It's usually helpful to create a document file to store these items if you are dealing with an extensive process such as warranty issue, banking error, or an insurance claim. Again, don't rely on the company to keep records for you. Be your own advocate.

Given these tips, let's consider how you might approach a situation assertively when your product is in need of repair, but is recently out of warranty. In this situation, let's say your dishwasher is broken, but is six months out of the labor warranty. It's going to cost you $75 just for the repairman to come to your home to find out what is wrong. What you need is a dishwasher that will work. You want the manufacturer to pay for the labor costs of the repair, as the parts are still covered by the warranty.

To communicate assertively with the company, you could call their customer service number. You would then use assertive language to explain what you need (a dishwasher repair) and what you want (the company to pay for the labor costs of the repair). Your side of the conversation could go like this: "Hello, may I have your name please? Thank you. I'm having a problem with my dishwasher and will need a repair. Yes, I realize that this product is out of warranty. I'm disappointed that it is having a problem when I've owned it for less than two years. I've called you today because I've been a loyal customer to your brand: I own four other appliances from your company. I am requesting that your company help pay for the repair. Yes, I realize the parts are covered under warranty. My concern is the labor costs. I want your company to pay for the cost of the labor to repair the dishwasher. I am willing to pay for the service call."

In the above example, you used the following assertive communication assets:

- You were respectful and got the representative's name.

- You stated right away what your need was.

- You emphasized the fact that you have been a loyal customer to the company.

- You then clearly stated that you want the company to pay for the labor portion of the repair.

- Your tone throughout was calm and clear.

Now let's look at the same scenario with a passive communication style:

"Hi, I think my dishwasher has something wrong with it. Oh, I didn't know it was that old. Can you do anything? No? Well, I'm very disappointed."

The lackadaisical attitude of this passive conversation shows that this person:

- Lacked respect—He or she just forged ahead with stating the problem and didn't ask the name of the representative. This could prove to be a mistake if that information is needed later.

- Didn't prepare very well for the conversation—He or she didn't know the age of the dishwasher or what specific service he or she needed or wanted; the caller just wanted just wanted "anything."

- Did not assert disappointment further—He or she could have continued to insist on an unwillingness to take an inflexible "no," and asked what the company "could" do. Instead, the caller gave up, gave in and didn't resolve the problem.

An aggressive personality is only concerned with getting what he or she wants by any means necessary. The aggressive communicator might say this:

"Yeah, I've got a repair person here right now and he says that this repair on my dishwasher is going to cost me $150 dollars. That's almost half of what I paid for it! I don't care that it's out of warranty. Your company should have made a better product! What are you going to do about it? Because if you don't pay for this repair, I want your supervisor right now so I can explain the rotten job that you're doing helping me!"

This person is so aggressive that:

- He or she is showing little to no respect for the company representative, but instead is angry and shouting from the start.

- He or she is demanding what an agreement without giving the representative a chance to speak or ask questions.

- He or she is escalating the situation by asking for a supervisor and making threatening comments to the representative without giving the person a chance to provide assistance.

You can imagine how difficult it can be to get anything accomplished when approaching this situation with passive or aggressive behaviors and communications.

Look at your problem from the perspective of the company representative. Just imagine what it must be like for this person, having to talk to five or even fifteen aggressive, angry customers. You'd want to talk to someone respectful, too! You don't have to become this person's friend. You just want the company representative to be your ally in whatever matter you're trying to resolve, and treating that person with respect is a great way to begin.

Passive consumers aren't sure of what they want and aren't willing to work to get it. Aggressive customers focus only on pushing others around and usually run out of communication tools as soon as they lose patience. The assertive consumer can best be described as someone who knows what he or she wants and is willing to pursue it respectfully and persistently. If you use assertive communication, you will have an armory of tools at your disposal.

Maintain your poise and dignity. Get what you need and want. If you respectfully, assertively communicate as a consumer, you're much more likely to be satisfied with your purchase or resolution to your problem.

CHAPTER 6 - RAISING ASSERTIVE CHILDREN

It's always too early to quit.—
Norman Vincent Peale

Earlier, we discussed how parents can use assertiveness in their communication with children as well as how to teach children to have respect for their parents. In this chapter, we discuss how to raise assertive children.

Teaching your children to be assertive gives them several critical life skills. For starters, if your children can become assertive, respectful communicators at a young age, they are less likely to be bullied by other kids or lured into dangerous situations by strangers. Children want to be liked by adults and peers; therefore, it may be very difficult for them to say "no" to someone (even respectfully) because they fear potential rejection. Assertive communication can teach your children that saying "no" to someone does not necessarily lead to rejection, and more importantly, may keep them safe from dangerous situations. Consider assertive communication another tool your children can use to help them navigate the world safely.

Moreover, assertive skills build self-esteem. Children with low self-esteem may fall into the trap of believing that their opinions don't matter and aren't worth expressing. When you teach your child to be assertive, he or she learns that his or her thoughts and feelings are important. The child also learns how to express these feelings in a respectful way. This process gives children the self-confidence to think and act for themselves instead of allowing others to influence their behaviors.

You can teach children to be assertive using the same exercises discussed in Chapter 2—by role-playing with them. To role-play, start by creating scenarios of peer pressure, bullying, or even of a child predator trying to lure the child. Then discuss with your child how he or she should respond to each situation. Afterwards, play the role of the bully and have your child practice the responses you two discussed.

An important tool in your child's assertive arsenal is the word "no." When role-playing with your child, emphasize that he or she has that basic right to say "no" and mean it without having to apologize or explain further.

For example, if you are teaching your young one to handle a bully at school, you might role play the following conversation: "Hey, stupid! Yeah, I'm talking to you! What's your problem? Get over here now!" You would then encourage your child to practice saying, "No, you can't treat me that way. Leave me alone." In a more extreme example, such as with a child predator, the child is to yell loudly, "No!" and get away from that person as quickly as possible.

This ensures the other person knows that the child doesn't accept the aggressive advance.

Talk calmly, yet frankly to your children about dangerous situations. Give them specific steps such as saying "no" to someone who is asking them to do something they know is wrong. When someone offers them drugs or makes a sexual or an aggressive advance, this one word, "no," and their ability to use it can give them the confidence they will need to walk away and go to an adult for help.

Beyond teaching your child to say "no," you can teach him or her clear, respectful ways to handle less dangerous situations like a disagreement with a friend. For example, you could role play with the child and suggest that you are a friend he or she has had a fight with. You could teach the child to say, "Jill, I don't like it when we fight. I want us to be friends again. Please don't call me names." This is an extremely simplistic, yet clear message that children of all ages can grasp.

Parents can teach in two ways: One is by telling their children what to do; the other is modeling what they should do. Both can be very effective, but when it comes to assertive communication, it pays to remember that children usually watch what you do more than they listen to what you say. The U.S. Department of Health suggests that, "One of the most important things a parent or caring adult can do is model good behavior." It's up to you as a parent to utilize your best assertiveness skills to teach your children how to react appropriately in situations where conflict may arise.

One of the most prevalent places where your child will be able to observe your behavior is at home. If you cannot assert yourself effectively with your family, your children may learn that it is o.k. to be pushed around. If you can use assertive communication with your spouse or partner, even your youngest children can learn to model speaking with respect and carrying themselves with dignity.

Outside of the home, you can model assertiveness in public situations. For example, if you're at a restaurant and your order isn't prepared correctly, you could say the following: "Excuse me, I ordered a salad with the dressing on the side. Unfortunately, this salad has dressing on it already. I'd like a new salad, please." This is concise, sets boundaries that say what you want, and is respectful of the server's feelings. You aren't yelling at or blaming them for the mistake; you are just pointing out the problem and asking for a resolution.

Whether you tell your child what to do or model those behaviors, you want to avoid the trap of becoming a "helicopter parent." A "helicopter parent" is one who hovers around the child just waiting for the opportunity to save him or her from conflict. This type of parent does not teach a kid much beyond the idea that the he or she is in need of constant rescue. The behavior doesn't teach assertive communication or creative problem-solving.

Let's look at a scenario where parents can help their young ones stand up for themselves respectfully. Your child is waiting for a turn on a swing at the park. Another child has been on the swing for a while and doesn't seem to be going anywhere soon. Should you:

A. Go over and tell the other kid that your child wants a turn and that it's time to get off.

B. Wait to see how your child responds to the situation and offer a suggestion as to what he or she could say only if your child asks for your help.

C. Tell your child it's time to leave because you don't want him or her to have a confrontation with the other one.

If you answered B, you not only recognized the assertive behavior; you realized that it isn't your place to resolve this problem for your adolescent. Answer A models aggressive communication, and answer C is a passive behavior. Answer B has the added benefit of teaching your child how to resolve problems. It can be difficult to "let go" and allow your child to make his or her own mistakes and decisions, but making mistakes is a critical part of learning and life.

When you teach your children to communicate assertively, you give them tools for their future that you may not have had at their age. In essence, you're giving them a wonderful new gift: You're teaching them to respect themselves, to get what they want out of life, and to respect others while they do it. These are traits that would make any parent proud.

CHAPTER 7 - MAKING
THE TRANSITION

You won't get people to hold back
their opinions just because you
suppress yours so you may as well
stand up & be counted
— Anonymous

Starting on a new path to assertiveness is not easy. In fact, it can be quite nerve racking, especially in the beginning. Old habits are difficult to change, even if those habits bring only pain and frustration. As a result, just because you know what to do and how does not mean that you should or will be able to do it. There are a lot of old fears, anxieties, and insecurities that can come up when you are in an actual assertive situation.

How well someone transitions will depend on the person. For some people, the transition will be easy. Some are at a place in their heads and lives where all they really needed was someone to understand what they were going through. That coupled with a little bit of guidance and vote of confidence is enough to transform them into new people who can go on to becoming successfully assertive individuals.

For others, the transformation will not be so instantaneous. Many will experience difficulty when starting out. They will have to read through the book a few times to understand what is being said. They will also have to go out and try the techniques and advice several times and in several different situations to get a sense for what assertiveness feels like. As long as these people stick with their efforts, they will begin to internalize the behavior. They will know what it looks like to go back and forth with a difficult person. As things click and as they receive the response and respect they desire, their success will give them additional motivation to continue.

Still, others will struggle. These people will know exactly what to do and how; they will be motivated to take action, and many times, they will go out the door ready for action, but they won't be able to follow through. They will walk into a situation and freeze up. They will have an entire argument for their boss or customer service representative prepared, but once they get in front of that person, they will buckle. If they don't buckle, what comes out of their mouth will be the exact opposite of what they intended to say.

I have to say that I feel for these individuals. I myself have been in their shoes. I wish I could write instructions that could make them skip this treacherous learning curve. Unfortunately, for some of us, this is the card we are dealt in life. As you work through the curve, it will appear as though the harder you try, the further back you are pushed. I also know, however, that by being persistent and practicing the skill every day, whether with minor issues like your server getting your order wrong or with bigger ones like an irrational family member, you will build yourself up. Slowly but surely, it will happen. The more you practice and the more you stay with it, the more assertive you will become.

Another aspect of the transition is that progress won't always be forward. As with any change, whether it is to lose weight, stop smoking, or learn a new skill, the path is never straight. You don't get on the road and walk until you reach your destination. You will encounter bypasses, diversions, and deviations. The route is more like a corkscrew where you move forward several steps, move back a few, move forward some more, then move back a little again.

That means that sometimes you'll be able to assert yourself, but other times you won't. Sometimes you will achieve big results. At other times you will achieve nothing. During the times you achieve nothing, it may seem like you are regressing or losing your touch. However, you are not.

Realize this is simply the development process. There is a lot of backward and side-to-side movement on the path to assertiveness. Be open to this. It will take away some of the frustration as you work to integrate assertiveness into your being. Do not feel that you are regressing and or losing your touch when you find yourself in a situation where you failed to defend your rights. The more you keep at it, the less you will move back.

Lastly, when you initially try to assert yourself, you may go overboard. Instead of acting calmly; you may yell, be rude, or come off harsh in some way. This is also normal, especially in the beginning. When you've held yourself back for so long, you build a very strong and resistive wall. Such a wall requires a lot of force and intensity to break through. Since you have to use such force to push through, when you finally do it, you will be so charged with that force, it will carry into the conversation and interaction, making you to come off emotional, stimulated, and even aggressive. The longer you've held back regarding an issue or the longer you've allowed others to push you around, the stronger will be this initial response.

Again, this is part of the process of becoming an assertive individual. To get past the internal resistance that keeps you from speaking out, you will go overboard. And when you do, it will feel as though all your emotions, years of frustration, and anger are pouring over the cliff in that one interaction.

This is why we recommend that you practice. Practicing will not only help you work and flesh out your argument, it will ease you into the process and ensure you do not lash out, especially at someone important like your boss. For practice, follow the recommendations in chapter two. Repeat what you are going to say and do in front of the mirror. Rehearse with a friend and/or family member. You can even build up your skill by practicing with minor day-to-day issues that would not normally get you worked up, like a waitress mixing up your order. In these situations, don't worry about getting what you want. Simply focus on asserting yourself calmly and in the right way.

Another exercise to make the transition easier is to watch people who are strong, assertive communicators. We all have people in our lives that are gifted in this area, whether they are relatives, friends, acquaintances or passersby. These individuals have a knack for talking to and gaining others' respect. Look for these people in your environment and watch what they do and how they interact. You don't have to befriend or hang out with them (although this can help). All you have to do is observe the various ways they get into and out of conversations with people. See how they act, react, and maintain composure.

When doing this, observe as many different types of people as you can—young and old, men and women, attractive and unattractive, and even high and low status. In addition, perform the observations in as many different settings as possible—at the grocery store, office, library, and social gatherings. Identify and examine as many strong, assertive communicators in and around you.

Observing people in assertive interactions was very instrumental to my success. The more I observed others, the more I saw how it was done. I also noticed that assertiveness was independent of age, sex, and status. It was a matter of choice, and those who chose to assert did so without feeling bad about it. Those who didn't, simply watched from the sidelines. Most important of all, I saw that assertiveness was not at all that hard and rarely resulted in the consequences I feared and dreaded. All of this gave me tremendous insight as well as motivation to act.

These are some difficulties that may hold you back when starting on your assertive journey. Another factor that can hold you back relates to myths that we carry about assertiveness. Many of us have misperceptions that discourage assertive behavior. The Livestrong website does an exceptional job of addressing and diffusing these myths, which we've included below.

Myths that Discourage Assertive Behavior

"Myth 1, Anxiety: Some people believe that overt signs of anxious behavior indicate weakness or inadequacy. These individuals assume that if they were to exhibit anxiety, they would be ridiculed, rejected or taken advantage of by others. This is self-defeating, for the harder people try to camouflage anxious feelings, the harder it is to conceal the accompanying symptoms of trembling, sweating, flushing, etc.

One method of reducing anxiety is to acknowledge that anxious feelings are present. One may discover that others experience similar feelings under certain circumstances. If people can disclose their feelings of discomfort safely, they will find it unnecessary to expend so much energy disguising them; therefore, the anxiety will no longer interfere with the task at hand or impair their ability to cope in life.

Myth 2, Modesty: This myth consists of three parts:

1. The inability to acknowledge or say positive things about oneself

2. The inability to accept compliments from others

3. The inability to give compliments to others

Some people fear that positive self-statements seem egocentric. They fail to discriminate between the accurate representation of accomplishments and over exaggeration. Additionally, they may fear that once they assert themselves, they will have to live up to these expectations 100 percent of the time. Inability to self-disclose positively may hinder their opportunities. If they don't believe in themselves, it is unrealistic to expect others to believe in them.

People who are unable to receive compliments are indirectly damaging their self-respect. After several unsuccessful attempts, most people trying to give genuine compliments will hesitate, feeling uncomfortable in giving positive feedback. The intended recipient of the praise, no longer hearing positive feedback, may begin to question their self-worth.

Sometimes others may use insincere praise as a manipulative tool ("You are such a great worker; by the way, could you cut the lawn.") However, assuming that all positive feedback is insincere, manipulative or misleading will hinder both the development of a healthy lifestyle and a positive self-concept. Positive feedback is a powerful tool in this sense.

Some people are unable to provide others with positive feedback. They may be unaware of the potential positive effects, e.g., greater rapport or satisfaction in life. Sometimes others have difficulty delivering praise because they fear making themselves vulnerable. They may be unable to elicit feelings easily and openly. Perhaps this is an alien behavior because they have never received positive feedback themselves. Or, maybe there is a risk involved in developing more honest, open relationships.

For whatever reason, modesty does not enhance mutually satisfying, spontaneous interpersonal relationships.

Myth 3, Good Friend: This myth assumes that others can read my mind based upon our past relationship, e.g.: "She should have known how I felt" or "My husband should have known how hard I have been working and given me Saturday morning free."

Lack of good, facilitative communication is apparent here. One must remember that individuals don't always respond in the same manner to the same situation.

This type of expectation will undoubtedly lead to guilt, resentment, hurt feelings and misunderstanding within a relationship, assuming that others have known you long enough to know your mind or how you are thinking.

Myth 4, Obligation: This myth indicates that some people disregard their personal needs and rights due to a belief in personal obligations to others. These people put others ahead of themselves. Obviously the others' needs cannot always be met; however, those who routinely neglect to express their needs and rights, and who find themselves imposed upon quite frequently, are being restrained by this belief in the myth of obligation. They are often unable to make requests of others they project that others feel the obligation to meet their needs, too.

This myth, along with the others, facilitates neither self-respect nor the development of open, healthy relationships.

Myth 5, Gender role myths: Sometimes people behave in a particular manner due to various gender role expectations. This has been especially true for women. Is it feminine to be assertive or outspoken? The myth of obligation fits into this category, too. Due to erroneous expectations, many women are unable to refuse requests, even unreasonable ones. This may be true regardless of whether the request would interfere with their needs and rights.

Men have been encouraged to act upon their needs and rights aggressively, to fill the "macho" or controlling role in a relationship. Gender role expectations can color behavior, often to the opposite extreme. Some men may be inappropriately passive, while social pressures often call for men to take an aggressive stand.

Gender role expectations limit people's options for acting appropriately upon their beliefs, needs and rights. They close the door to spontaneous, sincere interactions.

Myth 6, Strength of an issue: It is sometimes risky to take a stand, even on issues about which people might feel quite strongly. It may be interpreted as pressuring others to accept one's beliefs, especially when discussing a controversial issue. People may not choose to take the risk of alienating themselves from others.

People who cannot discuss their beliefs assertively are closing the door to honest expression. The opportunity for a potentially stimulating exchange, which may afford them an opportunity for self-growth, will not happen."

These are myths that often keep people from taking a healthy stance. If they've kept you from taking a stance in the past, it's time to change that. Again, this is a process that takes time, care, and practice. It may help to begin by looking at one area, such as anxiety, that really is difficult for you and tackling it first.

CONCLUSION - YOUR NEW TOOLKIT

If liberty means anything at all, it
means the right to tell people what
they do not want to hear
.—George Orwell

When you began listening to this audiobook, you may have had a passive personality, but a strong desire to change. Now you have a toolkit of new skills and information to utilize as you become a more assertive communicator. With your new toolkit, you're equipped with information and exercises to:

- **Physically present yourself as someone to be considered seriously.** You have exercises you can practice whenever you find yourself having a hard time looking someone in the eye or standing up tall to speak in front of a crowd.

- **Ensure that the person who you believe to be matches the person that others see.** You present your inner thoughts clearly, respectfully, and concisely without apologizing for who you are or what you are saying.

95

- **Communicate with precision**. You have four different, yet specific methods, learned in Chapter 2, to articulate yourself in nearly any situation. You now know how to use your voice correctly so that you'll avoid being misunderstood or ignored.

- **Be a better partner to your significant other**. You learned that communication is most effective when you clearly explain your wants and needs rather than assuming that the other person will just know what you want. You also learned that being an active listener will improve your chances of having your needs and wants met.

- **Be a better parent**. Now that you know how to hold your ground, you can teach this valuable skill to your children. You can talk to them about assertive behavior or model it in everyday situations, so they can learn to respect themselves and others early in their development.

- **Be a better friend or caretaker to a parent**. You are prepared to deal with difficult challenges that arise as an adult and are better able to set boundaries, admit that you need help, and ask questions.

- **Handle workplace challenges**. You have tools to help you stand up for yourself when you want recognition or a higher salary. You're better able to say "no" when someone tries to overburden your schedule or take advantage of your time.

- **Shop savvy and get what you need as a consumer**. You have new ground rules to help when faced with a challenging situation that calls for fortitude and persistence. You also have more effective ways to deal with high-pressure sales people.

• **Change your mindset**. By using these tools, your mindset will begin to change from a passive victim to an in-control communicator. The more you employ the tools, the more you will see yourself that way. Eventually, the title will become a self-fulfilling prophecy.

Measuring Your Success

The rewards of assertive communication are many. Here are a few general areas where you're likely to notice improvements right away.

• **You don't feel as stressed**. Having to give in all the time is painful. It's ego-bruising and can make you think you don't matter. Conflicts of any size may have made you feel anxious or even nauseous. When you call up that strength to communicate assertively, even though your heart may be racing, you'll feel relieved for saying what you want. You may even feel giddy for finally being able to say "no" to something you've been dreading.

• **Your relationships become more honest**. There are no guarantees that you'll get what you want when you communicate assertively. However, what is guaranteed is that the other person will know exactly what you want and need if you've been assertive and respectful. You aren't pretending anymore. You are being a genuine, respectful partner/parent/friend/employee who's fully empowered to set boundaries and express yourself honestly.

- **Your physical health improves**. Being constantly passive may be a symptom of a deeper problem like low self-esteem or depression. Being angry all the time with aggressive behavior has likely raised your blood pressure or given you a headache or two. When you're assertive, you're in control of your emotions and what you're saying and doing. You don't feel guilty or upset about communicating because you are respecting yourself and the other person as well. You don't have to feel afraid or feel that you have to yell when faced with conflict. You may find this refreshing turn of events leads to a quieter mind, better rest at night, lower blood pressure, and more energy throughout your day.

Whatever benefits you gain from your new assertive behavior, don't let your previous passive limitations overshadow them. Remember this sage advice from Dennis Waitley: "Learn from the past, set vivid, detailed goals for the future, and live in the only moment of time over which you have any control: now."

I am happy to see that you have read this far. I hope you found the material useful and gained valuable insight on developing yourself into a stronger and better communicator.

Please make sure to download your free book *Assertive at Work: Thriving in a Workplace of Mind Games and Bullies* and receive regular tips and reminders about keeping up with your new found assertive behavior. You can download the free copy at www.ScaredCocoon.com/free.

Lastly, with the success of this book, many have copied and plagiarized the material in here. Visit **www.ScraredCocoon.com/review** for examples.

In addition to copying, these authors post damaging reviews to boost their own sales. It takes time to address each issue, and often, it doesn't get resolved.

I believe the best solution is to take the high road and continue growing reviews. With that, if you like what you have read, I politely and ***assertively*** ask that you take a moment to leave a review where you made the purchase.

It takes less than a minute and can be as short as "I like this book" or "I found it useful," though your efforts will protect legitimate authors while maintaining integrity in the industry.

To leave a review, simply:

1. Visit **Scaredcocoon.com/review**

2. Click the appropriate link

3. Write a few words

Cheers to you for taking control of the now. Live assertively and create the life you want!

Made in the USA
Las Vegas, NV
12 July 2021